CHICAGO, 1968

REACTING TO THE PAST is an award-winning series of immersive role-playing games that actively engage students in their own learning. Students assume the roles of historical characters and practice critical thinking, primary source analysis, and argument, both written and spoken. Reacting games are flexible enough to be used across the curriculum, from first-year general education classes and discussion sections of lecture classes to capstone experiences, intersession courses, and honors programs.

Reacting to the Past was originally developed under the auspices of Barnard College and is sustained by the Reacting Consortium of colleges and universities. The Consortium hosts a regular series of conferences and events to support faculty and administrators.

Note to instructors: Before beginning the game you must download the Gamemaster's Materials, including an instructor's guide containing a detailed schedule of class sessions, role sheets for students, and handouts.

To download this essential resource, visit https://reactingconsortium.org/games, click on the page for this title, then click "Instructors Guide."

CHICAGO, 1968

Policy and Protest at the Democratic National Convention

Nicolas W. Proctor

BARNARD

The University of North Carolina Press

Chapel Hill

The University of North Carolina Press has been a member of the Green Press Initiative since 2003.

Cover illustration: *Young "Hippie" Standing in Front of a Row of National Guard Soldiers, Across the Street from the Hilton Hotel at Grant Park, at the Democratic National Convention in Chicago, August 29, 1968*. Warren K. Leffler, photographer. Courtesy Library of Congress.

ISBN 978-1-4696-7070-6 (pbk.: alk. paper)
ISBN 978-1-4696-7237-3 (e-book)

ABOUT THE AUTHOR

NICOLAS W. PROCTOR received his PhD from Emory University and is a Professor of History at Simpson College, where he has served as department chair and director of the first-year program. He has received all three of the college's major faculty awards: the Faculty Award for Campus Leadership in 2016, the Distinguished Teaching Award in 2006, and the Faculty Research Award in 2003.

After completing a traditional monograph, *Bathed in Blood: Hunting and Mastery in the Old South*, he reoriented his research to fit the needs of a teaching institution and focused on writing historical role-playing games. He has published two of these with Reacting to the Past: *Kentucky, 1861: Loyalty, State, and Nation*, which he wrote with Margaret Storey, and *Forest Diplomacy: Cultures in Conflict on the Pennsylvania Frontier, 1757.*

To help game authors, he wrote a *Game Designer's Handbook*. He also currently chairs the Reacting Consortium's editorial board, which oversees the development of hundreds of games. He is working on a game about the Reconstruction era in Louisiana after the Civil War. He lives in Des Moines, Iowa, with his family, many pets, a print shop, lots of books, and too many Legos.

CONTENTS

3. THE GAME

4. ROLES AND FACTIONS

CHICAGO, 1968

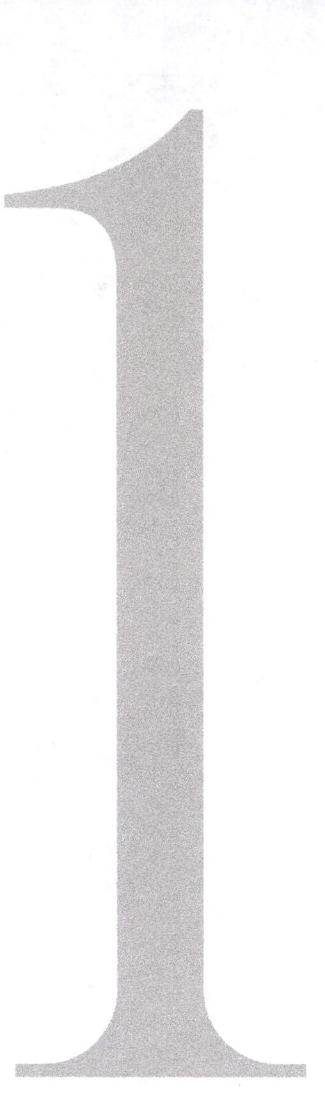

PART 1: INTRODUCTION

BRIEF OVERVIEW OF THE GAME

On August 26, 1968, delegates to the Democratic National Convention gathered in Chicago to decide upon the details of their platform and to nominate a candidate for president, but their party was deeply divided. They disagreed about domestic policy and the war in Vietnam. Members of the party's liberal contingent generally supported continued emphasis on civil rights and an end to the war. Meanwhile, conservative Democrats—particularly those from the South—argued the opposite. Given Alabama governor George Wallace's departure from the party and the announcement of his presidential candidacy as an Independent, the conservative wing was hard to ignore. Each of these groups sought to win over the moderate center of the party.

As party delegates debated policy in Chicago's International Amphitheatre, crowds of protesters descended upon the city to have their voices heard. Many lacked firm political convictions, but others were dedicated and experienced political activists. Antiwar protesters planned to use the methods of the civil rights movement—sit-ins and protest marches—to bend the party to their will. It was unclear how well they would work with the absurdist Yippies, who, determined to make a mockery of the Convention, intended to nominate a pig for president. Other, more militant, protesters saw the unrest in Chicago as the seedbed for true revolution. They saw the entire system as corrupt, so they welcomed the wrath of the Chicago Police Department; they hoped to show the American people the corruption of their ruling institutions.

Journalists flooded the city to cover the stories created by delegates and protesters. Many were professional, mainstream journalists who worked for big city dailies like the *New York Times*, established news magazines like *Time*, and television networks like CBS. The potential for chaos drew less mainstream, "underground" journalists like flies to honey.

Over the course of this game, as a result of the interactions between these different agendas and points of view, players will develop a better understanding of the complexities of the social and cultural tumult that has come to be known as "the Sixties."

PROLOGUE FROM TWO PERSPECTIVES

The following vignettes ask you to imagine yourself in Chicago at the beginning of the opening of the Democratic Convention. The first is from the point of view of one of the straightlaced convention delegates. The second is told by a young and recently radicalized protester.

I. Welcome, Democrats!

The taxi drivers are on strike, so you, along with dozens of other delegates to the Democratic National Convention, board a charter bus in front of Chicago's massive Conrad Hilton Hotel. You are thrilled to be staying in the same hotel as most of the major candidates. Several have booked entire floors for their staff and supporters. Eugene McCarthy is on the fifteenth. Hubert Humphrey is way up on the twenty-sixth. He's the vice president, so you guess this makes sense.

You appreciate the attention to security. Police officers are everywhere. You have seen the silhouettes of federal agents on the roof and dark-suited men prowling the corridors of the hotel. Apparently, photographers have been warned not to take pictures through open windows lest they be mistaken for snipers. That seems excessive, but given what happened to Martin Luther King Jr. and the Kennedy boys, maybe not.

In anticipation of the Convention, Mayor Daley spent over $500,000 sprucing up his city. You see evidence of this in the gleaming silver paint on the guardrails as your bus speeds along the Dan Ryan Expressway, but there is no covering up the dingy, high-rise public housing to either side as you ride south toward Chicago's International Amphitheatre—the site of the Convention itself.

As you drive past a building with smoke stains above several boarded-up windows, your seatmate, a taciturn delegate from Iowa, looks concerned. In the wake of King's assassination, Chicago's south side was wracked by forty-eight hours of rioting, which some prefer to call an uprising. Many buildings were set on fire. When firefighters responded, some of them were shot at. In response, Mayor Daley issued a "shoot to kill" order to police. During the riots, eleven were killed, ninety police officers were injured, over two thousand were arrested, and over two hundred buildings were seriously damaged. Things only settled down after President Johnson dispatched units of the regular army to restore order. In the aftermath, the city simply bulldozed many of the damaged buildings.

Daley's efforts to spruce up the city become more evident after you exit the expressway and enter the neighborhood around the amphitheatre. Bright-red fire hydrants and Kelly green lampposts line the way. Wooden fences, painted an array of soothing colors, conceal empty lots and junkyards. There are no other vehicles. The Chicago police have closed the street to traffic.

The International Amphitheatre has become a fortress. Streets are blocked off, police are posted on the roof, barbed wire defends the western perimeter, and special identification cards are required to enter the building. Police helicopters hover overhead. Two thousand Chicago cops and one thousand federal agents patrol the area. The city's 11,500-man force is on twelve-hour shifts, so there is no shortage of personnel. In addition, over five thousand riot-trained members of the Illinois National Guard have been called up for duty. Five thousand more are on alert. "No one," Mayor Daley has vowed, "is going to take over the streets." You believe him.

Still, protesters are tricky people. One of the worst, an anarchist named Yippie Abbie Hoffman, has promised to slip LSD—a potent and highly illegal hallucinogen—into the Chicago water supply. You turn to the Iowan and ask, "What's going to happen if they put dope in the water?"

"Daley has it covered," he replies confidently. "He put men on every filtration plant and pumping station. Twenty-four hours a day." He pauses and adds, "Welcome to Fort Daley."

The amphitheatre is right next to Chicago's vast stockyards. Once you exit the bus, you realize that Chicago is not called the "hog butcher to the world" for nothing. The odor of manure, urine, and blood is intense. It is not improved by the August heat. Despite the stench as you enter the building, you feel a thrill. This is a historical moment. But then you stumble. Maybe it is *that kind* of historical moment.

II. Journey to the Festival of Life

Rather than attend the Convention, you and your fellow protesters are going to disrupt it. The delegates are unthinking, heedless idiots, which is why you are headed to Chicago in a van with three other members of the Resistance. In many ways, this is a little surprising to you. Until eleven months ago you were completely apolitical.

This changed when the draft board started breathing down your boyfriend's neck. By last October, he was cornered and ready to volunteer in the hope of a posting to Germany. You argued that he should evade the draft by moving to Canada. Frustrated by his refusal to do so, and unwilling to accept defeat, you went to Washington, D.C., for the march on the Pentagon—the largest antiwar demonstration to date. If he would not save his life, you would save it for him.

When you joined tens of thousands of other protesters on the National Mall, you realized that you were not alone in your determination to end the war—far from it. The size of the crowd and the poor quality of the PA system prevented you from hearing most of the speeches, which was a hassle, but you still felt something: you felt like you were part of a *movement*. You rode high for a few hours, buoyed by thoughts of peace and love and some mighty fine marijuana, but then the U.S. marshals moved in. The sight of them clubbing demonstrators lit something inside of you.

It was not just about you and your boyfriend any more. It was about justice. It was about saving America from blind, fascist scumbags like LBJ who squander innocent lives in pursuit of meaningless slogans and abstract concepts. You came home with your consciousness raised. Your boyfriend did not share your growing spirit of radicalism, so you dumped him and found new friends.

You met Victor at the march. It's his van. He worked on voter registration drives in South Carolina and was already radicalized when he came to Washington. He dropped out of his graduate program in order to devote himself to the movement, but his commitment is leavened by a sense of absurdity. During the protest, he chanted along when they tried to levitate the Pentagon. Of course, it did not work. Victor did not care. He thought it was a gas.

Victor is tall and has a pointy beard. In a war-surplus helmet and ratty leather jacket, he cuts a dashing figure. He considers himself a Yippie. In Chicago, they plan to nominate a candidate for president: Pigasus, a twenty-two-pound pig purchased from a local farmer. A few days ago on Civic Center Plaza, some of the Yippies who are already in Chicago announced his candidacy. The Chicago police were not amused. They arrested seven and took Pigasus to the Humane Society. "It's cool," Victor said with a laugh. "Illinois has plenty of pigs."

Another one of your companions, Karl, an intense 20-year-old poet-actor-cab driver, thinks this sort of action is distracting. He is a member of the National Mobilization Committee to End the War in Vietnam, or the "Mobe." He is one serious cat. He's dedicated to ending the war through nonviolence and thinks the Mobe is the only antiwar group with the organizational ability to pull off a major demonstration.

He thinks the Hippies are useless and often mumbles things like, "Weaving macramé never ended any war." He thinks the Yippies like Victor are even worse; he thinks their antics will distract from serious issues. You are glad Karl is driving *and* committed to nonviolence. Otherwise, he and Victor would doubtless have traded some punches by now.

Maya, your third companion, is a member of Students for Democratic Society. You do not know much about that group, but over the past year, chapters of SDS have popped up on college and university campuses across the nation. Maya remains enrolled in college, but has not been in a classroom for months. Instead, she committed herself to bringing down the Establishment. She is also good friends with an herb named Mary Jane, and that's cool. Broad-shouldered and funny, she rolls a tight joint.

She's also into being prepared. Since you got on the road, she has been reading and rereading a special Convention issue of *Rat*, a New York underground newspaper. Before heading out, she made sure to pack plenty of Vaseline to protect your skin from mace, sheets of canvas for sleeping in the parks, and $200 in bail money. She has also been reading Mao's *On Guerilla Warfare*. This is a little troubling, but she assures you that it is "totally far out."

Maya admires SDS leader Tom Hayden, who traveled to North Vietnam last year. He has been outspoken about his plans for the protests, stating, "We are coming to Chicago to vomit on the politics of joy, to expose the secret decisions, upset the nightclub orgies, and face the Democratic Party with its illegitimacy and criminality." Right on!

On the way to Chicago, you mostly talked politics: the 1964 Berkeley Free Speech Movement, civil rights work in the South, the strike and occupation by students at Columbia University and Barnard College. You also talked about Karl's groovy poetry, but when you probed it for deeper meanings, he recoiled. "It's not supposed to say anything except what it says, man!" Then, after reflecting, he added, "I'm being evocative; not everybody can understand that, dig?"

When you get to Chicago, Maya is looking forward to getting trained in various resistance techniques. She is particularly excited to learn the "snake dance" used by Japanese student protesters that they are teaching in Lincoln Park. This led her to challenge Karl's commitment to nonviolent resistance. She thinks remaining passive in the face of escalating police brutality is foolish and degrading. On more than one occasion, their disagreements have ended with her yelling, "The pigs will never respect you until you can defend yourself!"

Throughout these talks, Victor always insists that there is no real difference between Republican nominee Richard M. Nixon and Democratic heir-apparent Vice President Hubert H. Humphrey. Victor enjoys making authoritative declarations like, "He would just deal superficially with the problems that liberals have historically engaged but have routinely failed to address in a meaningful and systematic way." Sometimes he sounds like a square who should go back to graduate school, but then he makes a funny face and cracks you up. He's cool.

After arriving in the city, you exited the expressway and drove toward the International Amphitheatre. You wanted to check out the fortifications around the convention site. As you drove through the neighborhood, the stench from the stockyards became overpowering. Maya asked, "Why did they decide to hold it here? This is the most god-awful place in the world."

After a few blocks, the police turned you back. At this point, your confidence dropped. You all realized that you did not have a clear idea about what was going to happen next. Mayor Daley has forbidden demonstration marches and even refused to give permission to camp in Lincoln Park. You are not sure what you are going to eat, or even where you are going to sleep. Maya breaks you out of your funk. She refuses to be intimidated. As Karl cranks the van around, she rolls down her window and shouts, "Get real, Daley! We're coming anyway!" The cops do not look amused.[1]

BASIC FEATURES OF REACTING TO THE PAST

Reacting to the Past is a series of historical role-playing games. After a few preparatory lectures, the game begins and the students are in charge. Set in moments of heightened historical tension, the games place you in the role of a person from the period. By reading the game book and your individual role sheet, you will find out more about your objectives, worldview, allies, and opponents. You must then attempt to achieve victory through formal speeches, informal debate, negotiations, and conspiracy. Outcomes sometimes differ from actual history; a postmortem session sets the record straight.

The following is an outline of what you will encounter in Reacting and what you will be expected to do.

Game Setup

Your instructor will spend some time before the beginning of the game helping you to understand the historical context for the game. During the setup period, you will use several different kinds of material:

- The game book (from which you are reading now), which includes historical information, rules and elements of the game, and essential historical documents.
- A role sheet, which provides a short biography of the historical person you will model in the game as well as that person's ideology, objectives, responsibilities, and resources. Some roles are based on historical figures. Others are "composites," which draw elements from a number of individuals. You will receive your role sheet from your instructor.

In addition to the game book, you may also be required to read historical documents or books written by historians. These provide additional information and arguments for use during the game.

Read this material before the game begins. And just as important, go back and reread these materials throughout the game. A second reading while *in role* will deepen your understanding and alter your perspective. Once the game is in motion, your perspectives may change. This will make some ideas begin to look quite different. Students who have carefully read the materials and who know the rules of the game will invariably do better than those who rely on general impressions and uncertain memories.

Game Play

Once the game begins, class sessions are presided over by students. In most cases, a single student serves as some sort of presiding officer. The instructor then becomes the Gamemaster (GM) and takes a seat in the back of the room. Though they do not lead the class sessions, GMs may do any of the following:

- Pass notes.
- Announce important events (e.g., Sparta is invading!). Some of these events are the result of student actions; others are instigated by the GM.
- Redirect proceedings that have gone off track.

Instructors are, of course, available for consultations before and after game sessions. Although they will not let you in on any of the secrets of the game, they can be invaluable in terms of sharpening your arguments or finding key historical resources.

The presiding officer is expected to observe basic standards of fairness, but as a fail-safe device, most Reacting to the Past games employ the "Podium Rule," which allows a student who has not been recognized to approach the podium and wait for a chance to speak. Once at the podium, the student has the floor and must be heard.

Role sheets contain private, secret information which you are expected to guard. You are advised, therefore, to exercise caution when discussing your role with others. Your role sheet probably identifies likely allies, but even they may not always be trustworthy. However, keeping your own counsel and saying nothing to anyone is not an option. In order to achieve your objectives, you *must* speak with others. You will never muster the voting strength to prevail without allies. Collaboration and coalition building are at the heart of every game.

Some games feature strong alliances called *factions*. As a counterbalance, these games include roles called Indeterminates. They operate outside of the established factions, and while some are entirely neutral, most possess their own idiosyncratic objectives. If you are in a faction, cultivating Indeterminates is in your interest, since they can be persuaded to support your position. If you are lucky enough to have drawn the role of an Indeterminate you should be pleased; you will likely play a pivotal role in the outcome of the game.

Game Requirements

Students in Reacting practice persuasive writing, public speaking, critical thinking, teamwork, negotiation, problem-solving, collaboration, adapting to changing circumstances, and working under pressure to meet deadlines. Your instructor will explain the specific requirements for your class. In general, though, a Reacting game asks you to perform three distinct activities:

Reading and Writing. This standard academic work is carried on more purposefully in a Reacting course, since what you read is put to immediate use, and what you write is meant to persuade others to act the way you want them to. The reading load may have slight variations from role to role; the writing requirement depends on your particular course. Papers are often policy statements, but they can also be autobiographies, battle plans, newspapers, poems, or after-game reflections. Papers provide the foundation for the speeches delivered in class.

Public Speaking and Debate. In the course of a game, almost everyone is expected to deliver at least one formal speech from the podium (the length of the game and the size of the class will determine the number of speeches). Debate follows. It can be impromptu, raucous, and fast-paced. At some point, discussions must lead to action, which often means proposing, debating, and passing a variety of resolutions. Gamemasters may stipulate that students must deliver their papers from memory when at the podium, or may insist that students wean themselves from dependency on written notes as the game progresses.

Wherever the game imaginatively puts you, it will surely not put you in the classroom of a twenty-first-century American college. Accordingly, the colloquialisms and familiarities of today's college life are out of place. Never open your speech with a salutation like "Hi guys" when something like "Fellow citizens!" would be more appropriate.

Always seek allies to back your points when you are speaking at the podium. Do your best to have at least one supporter second your proposal, come to your defense, or admonish inattentive members of the body. Note-passing and side conversations, while common occurrences, will likely spoil the effect of your speech; so you and your supporters should insist upon order before such behavior becomes too disruptive. Ask the presiding officer to assist you. Appeal to the Gamemaster as a last resort.

Strategizing. Communication among students is an essential feature of Reacting games. You will find yourself writing emails, texting, attending out-of-class meetings, or gathering for meals on a fairly regular basis. The purpose of frequent communication is to lay out a strategy for achieving your objectives, thwarting your opponents, and hatching plots to ensnare individuals troubling to your cause. When communicating with a fellow student in or out of class, always assume that he or she is speaking to you in role. If you want to talk about the "real world," make that clear.

Amid the plotting, debating, and voting, always remember that a Reacting game is only a game—resistance, attack, and betrayal are not to be taken personally, since game opponents are merely acting as their roles direct.

Counterfactuals

To maximize discussion, the organization of the Convention is simplified. Some issues that were decided in committees (particularly the credentialing committee and the platform committee) will be debated on the floor. In terms of the domestic policy elements of the platform, the delegates must work to focus the party's message, which is something that did not happen in 1968. The historical platform sprawled. The debate over the Vietnam plank offers a larger array of options than was historically the case at the Convention.

The order in which speeches are scheduled to take place in the Convention is intended to illuminate specific ideas rather than to resemble the historical pacing of the Convention.

Historically, Senator Edward "Ted" Kennedy did not attend the Convention, but including him as a player keeps his potential candidacy in play.

For ease of play, votes are allocated to individual players rather than distributed to states. This creates a higher level of indeterminacy than was present at the historical Convention.

To facilitate interactions, protesters and delegates are physically divided, but they occupy the same room. In addition, delegates who speak from the podium may be questioned from the floor by their fellow delegates or journalists.

PART 2: HISTORICAL BACKGROUND

CHRONOLOGY

November 1967	Eugene McCarthy announces his candidacy for the Democratic nomination.
January 1968	Tet offensive begins in South Vietnam.
February 1968	Orangeburg Massacre. Police kill three black students and injure twenty-eight during a protest against a segregated bowling alley in South Carolina.
	Richard Nixon announces his candidacy for the Republican nomination.
	George Wallace leaves the Democratic Party and announces his candidacy as an Independent.
	Kerner Commission report issued.
March 1968	McCarthy does well against President Lyndon Johnson in the New Hampshire primary.
	Robert Kennedy announces his candidacy.
	Johnson halts the bombing of North Vietnam north of the 19th parallel and announces his decision to not seek reelection.
April 1968	Martin Luther King Jr. assassinated. Riots erupt in more than 100 cities.
	Johnson signs Civil Rights Act of 1968, which includes a federal anti-riot provision.
	Tet offensive ends with massive Communist casualties.
	Hubert Humphrey announces his candidacy.
May 1968	McCarthy defeats Kennedy in Oregon primary.
	Paris peace talks begin between the United States and North Vietnam.

June 1968	Kennedy wins the California primary and is assassinated.
August 1968	Nixon secures the Republican Party nomination.
	George McGovern announces his candidacy.
	5,000 Illinois National Guardsmen arrive in Chicago to bolster police forces.
	Soviet troops invade Czechoslovakia to crush the Prague Spring movement.
	Democratic National Convention begins.

THE UNRAVELING OF THE DEMOCRATIC PARTY

To understand the domestic and foreign policy issues being debated at the Democratic National Convention in Chicago, as well as the frustrations and tactics of the protesters who seek to disrupt it, you should develop a broad sense of recent events in the United States and Southeast Asia. This section includes information that would have been known by the roles that you are playing, so it will help you to understand their ideas, motivations, and frustrations with the state of American society in August of 1968.

Johnson's Great Society

In 1964, Democrat Lyndon B. Johnson defeated Republican Barry Goldwater for the presidency with 61.1 percent of the popular vote, the greatest landslide in U.S. presidential history. This gave Johnson the ability to press forward with an ambitious domestic policy agenda, featuring a broad array of federal programs he hoped would eliminate poverty and racial injustice. In size and scope, these initiatives, known as the "**Great Society**," rivaled Franklin D. Roosevelt's **New Deal**, which greatly expanded the federal government in the 1930s and '40s.

The **Great Society** refers to a wide array of federal programs that President Johnson intended to use to eliminate poverty and racial injustice in the United States.

The **New Deal** refers to an earlier array of federal programs created by Democratic president Franklin D. Roosevelt. They ushered in the era of "big government" that included a wide variety of federal regulations and public works projects.

Johnson was determined to lift millions out of poverty with new federal programs and massive domestic spending. His programs included the expansion of existing programs such as Social Security, an old age and unemployment insurance program, and Food Stamps, which provided coupons for purchasing basic food products, as well as increased federal involvement in education, which included entirely new programs in education like Head Start and Upward Bound, which were intended to help impoverished children.

He also pushed for new federal programs to support the arts like the National Endowment for the Humanities and the National Endowment for the Arts, which provided funding for artists and performers, as well as programs for the massive expansion of federal involvement in health care. The new Medicare program aided the elderly while Medicaid focused on the poor. Originally conceived of as part of the New Deal, these programs had been tangled up in Congress for decades, but Johnson secured their passage as one of the crowning achievements of the Great Society. Upon signing the Medicare act into law, he proudly commented:

> No longer will older Americans be denied the healing miracle of modern medicine. No longer will illness crush and destroy the savings that they have so carefully put away over a lifetime so that they might enjoy dignity in their later years. No longer will young families see their own incomes, and their own hopes, eaten away simply because they are carrying out their deep moral obligations to their parents.[2]

The Great Society also expanded federal funding of infrastructure and public housing, often under the heading of "urban renewal." Designed to provide economic stimulus, some of these programs also resulted in the destruction of poor neighborhoods, many of them Black, which were bulldozed to make way for new highways, airports, and sports arenas. In 1963, novelist James Baldwin commented that "urban renewal" often meant "Negro removal."

More divisively, Johnson moved forward with landmark civil rights legislation. Much of the opposition came from members of his own party who were committed to the maintenance of white supremacy and legal segregation—especially in the South. When leaders of the **civil rights movement**, including Martin Luther King Jr., staged a series of marches in Selma, Alabama, they were met with violence from the state and local police. Johnson used his influence in Congress to secure the passage of the Voting Rights Act of 1965, which prohibited racial discrimination in voting and voter registration and promised federal intervention in defense of Black involvement in politics at all levels. This followed the Civil Rights Act of 1964, which had outlawed discrimination based on race, color, religion, sex, or national origin. These acts were celebrated by white liberals and American Blacks, but they threatened to turn a majority of southern whites, who traditionally voted Democrat, against the party.

The **civil rights movement** refers to the generations-long struggle by African Americans to gain equal rights in the United States.

In early August, hope that these acts might usher in a new era of racial concord were shattered by the violence of the Watts riots in Los Angeles. Sparked by a minor incident, but fueled by poverty, hopelessness, and police racism, the riots lasted for six days. They resulted in massive destruction and thirty-four deaths, which initiated waves of violent unrest in cities across the nation. Rather than easing racial tensions, critics noted that the policies of the "Great Society" actually appeared to be increasing them.

The War in Vietnam

The United States began its military involvement in Southeast Asia in the 1950s when it supported French colonial authorities in their struggle against local insurgents who received support from Chinese Communists. After the withdrawal of the French in 1954, the United States supported the anticommunist government of South Vietnam. This support deepened during the Kennedy administration when the United States stepped up aid, sent military advisors, and expanded the operations of the Central Intelligence Agency.

President Johnson inherited the policies of his predecessor, John F. Kennedy. He accepted the **Domino Theory**, recognized the chronic instability of South Vietnam, and took steps to escalate the war.

The **Domino Theory** was the idea that if one nation in Southeast Asia fell to communism, it would lead to the collapse of its neighbors. For details, see "The Domino Theory" in the Core Texts section of this game book, p. 153.

Containment was the dominant U.S. strategy during the Cold War. It justified the use of a variety of anti-communist foreign policy efforts.

In August 1964, in reaction to a real and imagined encounter between U.S. and North Vietnamese warships off the coast of Vietnam, which Johnson used as evidence of communist aggression in the region, Congress passed the Gulf of Tonkin Resolution, giving the president authority to escalate the war in Vietnam without a formal declaration of war. Johnson, who subscribed to the Cold War strategy of **containment** and the concomitant Domino Theory, which mandated a vigorous defense against communism wherever in the world it attempted to advance, subsequently approved the steady escalation of the war. This included the bombing of communist North Vietnam and the deployment of hundreds of thousands of U.S. combat troops to fight the Communists. This included counterinsurgency operations against the Vietcong insurgents in South Vietnam, air strikes against the communist North, special operations in neighboring Laos and Cambodia, and a military buildup in Thailand and the Philippines.

In the 1964 election, when Johnson's Republican opponent, Barry Goldwater, called for the escalation of the war in Vietnam, Johnson famously replied, "We are not about to send American boys 9 or 10,000 miles away from home to do what Asian boys ought to be doing for themselves."[3] He said one thing and did another.

When he assumed the presidency, there were 16,000 military personnel in Vietnam; by 1967 the total reached 525,000. Although a majority of the troops that fought in Vietnam had volunteered for service, about one quarter of them were conscripted through the Selective Service Act. Due to a variety of **draft** deferments, poor and working-class men without college educations were overrepresented in this pool.

The **draft** refers to the peacetime conscription of men into the military through the Selective Service Act.

Throughout this buildup, Johnson attempted to downplay the war in favor of drawing attention to the programs of his beloved Great Society, but the inability of the United States to achieve victory, coupled with the corruption and ineffectiveness of the forces of South Vietnam, resulted in mounting criticism. Soon, Johnson could not leave the White House without facing protesters chanting, *Hey, hey, LBJ, how many kids did you kill today?* Still, many hoped that they could see the light at the end of the tunnel. (To get a better sense of Johnson's characterization of the war, read his speech "Peace without Conquest," which appears in the Core Texts section of this game book, p. 129.)

On January 30, 1968, Vietnamese Communists launched the Tet offensive during what had traditionally been a holiday ceasefire. This broad and well-coordinated series of attacks came as a surprise because American military officials had repeatedly insisted that the escalation of American military involvement was winning the war and that the Communists were in retreat.

Militarily, the operation was a defeat for the Communists. After initial success, they suffered severe casualties as their attacks were beaten back by U.S. and South Vietnamese forces. Despite this, the audacity of the offensive had a profound effect on the American public. Having been led to believe that the power of the Communists was largely broken, more Americans began questioning the ability of the United States to win the war.

On February 27, after returning to New York from a trip to Vietnam, CBS anchorman Walter Cronkite ended an on-air commentary by stating, "To say that we are mired in stalemate seems the only realistic, if unsatisfactory conclusion." Considered by some to be the most trusted man on television, Cronkite suggested an exit from the war, "not as victors, but as an honorable people who lived up to their pledge to defend democracy, and did the best they could."[4]

1968 Riots

While public opinion soured toward the president's Vietnam policy, things turned from bad to worse in America's cities. In response to urban riots in the summer of 1967, Johnson had appointed the Kerner Commission to answer three questions: *What happened? Why did it happen? What can be done to prevent it from happening again and again?*

The Commission's formal report, which was issued on February 29, 1968, said that the United States was "moving toward two societies, one black, one white—separate and unequal." This was accompanied by a powerful indictment of white society: "What white Americans have never fully understood but what the Negro can never forget—is that white society is deeply implicated in the ghetto. White institutions created it, white institutions maintain it, and white society condones it." (For more, see the excerpts from the National Advisory Commission on Civil Disorders in the Core Texts section of this game book, p. 85.)

The report's criticism of federal anti-poverty programs was hardly a ringing endorsement of the Great Society, but it still called for massive federal spending to break up Black ghettos that had formed as a result of legal and de facto segregation throughout the nation. While the Civil Rights Act of 1964 struck down the Jim Crow laws that institutionalized legal segregation in the South, they did little to alter practices in the rest of the country that forced Black people to live in cramped and often decrepit inner-city neighborhoods. Black people were further impoverished by practices like red-lining, which allowed banks to engage in predatory lending practices, housing covenants, which prevented Black citizens from moving to white neighborhoods, and the construction of school districts that corralled Black students into sub-standard public schools.

Their assessment seemed on the mark when, on April 4, civil rights leader Martin Luther King Jr., who had travelled to Memphis, Tennessee, in order to assist a strike by sanitation workers, was assassinated. His murder sparked riots in over 100 cities across the nation. Sixty-five thousand federal troops were activated; thirty-nine people were killed, and tens of thousands arrested.

The riots on the South Side of Chicago were some of the worst. They resulted in the deaths of around eleven people and caused massive property damage. To suppress them the city dispatched 10,500 Chicago police supplemented by 6,700 Illinois National Guard and 5,000 U.S. Army regulars, who had to be airlifted in from Texas. During the unrest, Mayor Richard J. Daley gave police the authority "to shoot to kill any arsonist or anyone with a Molotov cocktail [an improvised firebomb] in his hand . . . and . . . to shoot to maim or cripple anyone looting any stores in our city."[5] Daley's statement was polarizing. Forty-seven percent of Americans living in large cities approved of shooting looters, but 49 percent thought there must be a better way to deal with the problem.[6] A few days after the riots were suppressed, Chicago police brutally cleared antiwar demonstrators from the downtown Civic Center Plaza.

In the wake of the riots, on April 11, Johnson signed the Civil Rights Act of 1968, which primarily addressed housing discrimination—a huge problem in Chicago and one of the key issues identified by the *Kerner Report*—but astute observers also noted that it included a new federal anti-riot law, which made it a crime to cross state lines with the intent to incite a riot.

The Democratic Presidential Candidates of 1968

Thus, by early 1968, Johnson's political power appeared to have reached low ebb. Having already lost ground in the 1966 elections, the Democratic Party was being pulled apart by disagreements about the war, civil rights, and the programs of the Great Society. The party that had only recently enjoyed the greatest electoral majorities since the New Deal appeared to be floundering, but Johnson remained the natural choice for the presidential nomination.

Minnesota Senator Eugene McCarthy was the first to challenge him. He entered the race for the presidency as a peace candidate in November 1967. Initially, few saw him as a serious candidate, but growing public discontent and a determined grassroots campaign allowed him to surprise the nation when he almost defeated Johnson in the March 12 New Hampshire Democratic primary. Johnson, who was widely considered unbeatable, suddenly seemed vulnerable.

New York Senator Robert F. Kennedy had been weighing the possibility of entering the race. Long in the public eye as John F. Kennedy's younger brother and the attorney general of the United States, Kennedy was a major political force. Soon after the New Hampshire primary, emboldened by Johnson's weakness, he decided to throw his hat into the ring as an additional candidate for the nomination. Despite accusations of opportunism (particularly from McCarthy supporters), the charismatic brother of the slain president attracted a great deal of support from "Doves" who opposed the war. (To get a good sense of Kennedy's appeal to the antiwar movement, read his speech that appears in the Core Texts section of this game book, p. 106.)

NOTE

Doves opposed the war in Vietnam, while Hawks advocated a firm military response to communist expansionism.

Rattled by the power of McCarthy's appeal and Kennedy's decision, Johnson attempted to shift course in Vietnam. In the hope of facilitating negotiations with the Communists, he attempted to de-escalate the war by placing greater restrictions on the bombing of North Vietnam. In addition, to everyone's surprise, he announced his decision to withdraw from the presidential campaign in order to focus on the war. On March 31, Johnson stated, "I shall not seek, and I will not accept, the nomination of my party for another term as your President." Initially, this seemed to bear some fruit in the war effort. On May 3, the United States and North Vietnam agreed to start peace talks in Paris, but the negotiators—W. Averell Harriman and Xuân Thuỷ, respectively—soon reached an impasse when North Vietnam demanded a full halt to the bombing.

Johnson's decision to bow out gave Vice President Hubert H. Humphrey the opportunity to join the race for the presidential nomination as the third major candidate. As Johnson's heir apparent, Humphrey ran on the eight-year record of the Johnson presidency and appeared to favor continuing Johnson's policies, so he was supported by the prowar "Hawks" in the party. As a candidate, Humphrey attempted to build upon his legacy as a longtime supporter of the civil rights movement, and he promised to "be his own man," but he was hamstrung by the need to support the continuation of the policies of the Johnson White House—policies that he had no hand in crafting. Humphrey's room for political maneuvering was further limited by Johnson's influence as the head of the Democratic Party. Numerous "pledge delegates" to the Convention were controlled by Johnson. If Humphrey wanted to enjoy their support, he needed to comply with Johnson's wishes.

The Democratic field was also complicated by the candidacy of states' rights advocate George Wallace. The arch-segregationist former governor of Alabama had bolted from the Democratic Party on February 8 and decided to run as a candidate of the American Independent Party. Strong support for his candidacy in the Deep South threatened to break apart the Democratic Party, which relied upon white southern voters since the beginning of the twentieth century. On the day Wallace announced his candidacy, three Black students were killed by

South Carolina state troopers in Orangeburg, South Carolina. The students had gathered to demand the integration of a local bowling alley.

Lacking a realistic chance at victory, Wallace hoped to attract enough support to deny his major party opponents a clear majority, which would trigger the unusual constitutional solution of resolving the election in the U.S. House of Representatives. If this occurred, he hoped to trade his support to whichever candidate was willing to put an end to federal enforcement of the Civil Rights Act of 1964 and the Voting Rights Act of 1965. Usually associated with segregation and a "law and order" stance toward urban unrest, Wallace developed a full array of positions that included opposition to the continuation of Johnson's policies in Vietnam. He did, however, maintain his support for many of Johnson's Great Society programs—particularly Social Security and Medicare, which benefitted his working-class white constituents. (For more on George Wallace's positions, see his speech in the Core Texts section of this game book, p. 144.)

The field was crowded, but Kennedy proved a powerful campaigner, and he began to attract the support of idealists who were lukewarm in their support for McCarthy as well as liberals who were Humphrey's core constituency. After winning the California primary, he seemed to be headed for victory, but on June 5, 1968, like his brother John and Martin Luther King Jr. before him, he was shot by an assassin. He died the next day. The nation reeled.

The Antiwar Movement

As the Democrats geared up for their party's Convention, protesters began converging on Chicago. Although Black civil rights organizations decided to stay away from the Convention (partly because every important Black leader in Chicago was put under police surveillance), antiwar protesters who hoped to create a massive demonstration consciously drew from the Black freedom struggle. (The pieces by David Harris and Akmed Lorence that appear in the Core Texts section of this game book, pp. 113 and 116, are good examples of the antiwar position.)

The **Mobe,** or the National Mobilization Committee to End the War in Vietnam, was a coalition of antiwar organizations.

Nonviolent tactics were fully embraced by the National Mobilization Committee to End the War in Vietnam (**Mobe**). A coalition of antiwar groups, the Mobe had become active in the spring of 1967 when they simultaneously staged large, antiwar marches in New York City and San Francisco. Later that fall, the Mobe reprised these efforts with its March on the Pentagon. Organized by David Dellinger and Jerry Rubin, the event gathered around fifty thousand people for an antiwar rally. As part of the event, the Yippies attempted to levitate the Pentagon with positive mental energy. After that failed, thousands marched toward the Pentagon in a massive act of civil disobedience. Six hundred and fifty protesters were arrested.

Inspired by the Student Nonviolent Coordinating Committee (SNCC)—an increasingly radical civil rights organization dominated by young people—some antiwar activists increasingly contemplated truly revolutionary action. Foremost among these groups were Students for a Democratic Society (**SDS**). Critical of U.S. foreign policy, income inequality, big business, racial discrimination, and the established political parties, the SDS called for "participatory democracy" and a "program against poverty" when they issued their political manifesto, the Port Huron Statement, in 1962. (It is included in the Core Texts section of this game book, p. 135.) By 1967, the SDS had spread to hundreds of campuses across the country. It had also become significantly more radical. Rather than working "within the system" like the Mobe, SDS supporters increasingly argued that the entire system needed to be overthrown.

The **SDS**, or Students for a Democratic Society, was a radical student group. By August 1968, some members contemplated a turn toward violence.

The antiwar movement built upon other foundations as well. Among them were the Bohemian Beat Generation of post–World War II authors, who included Allen Ginsberg, William S. Burroughs, and Jack Kerouac. Rejecting American materialism, the Beats embraced experimental writing, drugs, and sexual liberation. The Beats influenced a particularly strong influence on **Yippies** like Abbie Hoffman, Jerry Rubin, and Paul Krassner. This group, which coalesced in late 1967, mocked the status quo with anarchic, antiauthoritarian street theater. In Chicago, the Yippies hoped to attract five hundred thousand people to a five-day Festival of Life in Lincoln Park. Their plans featured live music, skinny-dipping in Lake Michigan, positive thinking, free love, and lots of drugs. Unsurprisingly, the city of Chicago refused to issue them permits. (A profane interview with Hoffman is at the beginning of the Core Texts section of this game book, p. 69. Read it to get a sense of the disruptive potential of this anarchic group.)

The **Yippies**, or members of the Youth International Party, were an anarchic group of radicals dedicated to the absurdist critique of American society.

The Republicans Pick Nixon

As the Democrats prepared to hold their Convention in Chicago, the Republican Party concluded their own Convention in Miami Beach, Florida, which culminated in the nomination of Richard M. Nixon on the first ballot. The former vice president, who had lost the 1960 presidential race to John Kennedy, had won most of the state Republican primaries and defeated a host of challengers including Michigan governor George Romney, New York governor Nelson Rockefeller, and California governor Ronald Reagan. Strongly anticommunist, Nixon nonetheless remained vague about his planned policies toward Vietnam. He simply announced that his first foreign policy priority was to "bring an honorable end to the war in Vietnam."

In the midst of the Republican National Convention, riots (resulting in four deaths and hundreds of arrests) broke out in the Miami ghetto Liberty City. Nixon took advantage of the political moment and called for "law and order." His acceptance speech condemned urban riots as well as antiwar protests, which were becoming more common—and resonated with voters. He called on the "silent majority" of

The Most Important Problem

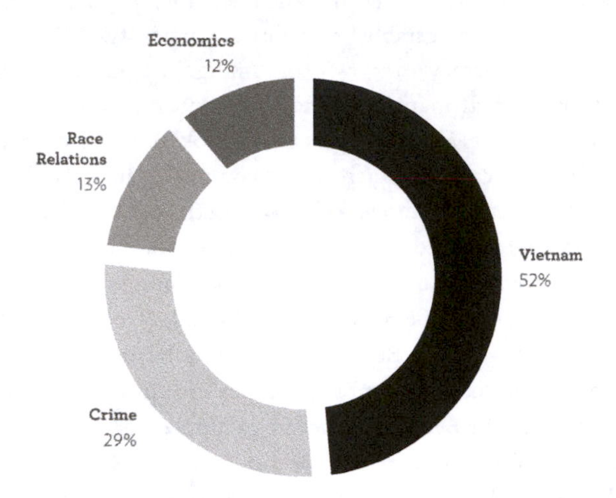

George H. Gallup, *The Gallup Poll: Public Opinion, 1935–1971* (Random House, 1972) 3: 2151. Note that some respondents picked more than one.

Americans, "the forgotten Americans, the non-shouters, the non-demonstrators," to support his campaign.

On August 4, just before the beginning of the Republican National Convention that preceded the Democratic Convention, a national Gallup poll asked Americans, "What do you think is the most important problem facing this country today?"[7] Some gave more than one answer, but their answers revealed a great deal about the concerns of the voters on the eve of the election. The results appear in the chart above. Nixon addressed all of these issues throughout his campaign, and he returned to them in his acceptance speech, but he sometimes used coded language and often remained purposefully vague about details. (To better understand Nixon's appeal, and the threat that he poses to the Democrats, read his acceptance speech, which appears in the Core Texts section of this game book, p. 74.)

Daley Fortifies Chicago

With its own convention fast approaching later in August, the Democratic Party was in disarray. In an attempt to rally what remained of Robert Kennedy's forces, South Dakota senator George S. McGovern, a moderate antiwar Democrat from the Midwest, formally announced his candidacy on August 10, 1968, just two weeks before the Convention. Searching for the Kennedy fire, many encouraged Robert's younger brother, Edward "Ted" Kennedy, to join the race as well. All the while, Governor Lester Maddox of Georgia, an outspoken white supremacist, entered the race in an attempt to stir up conservative Democrats who opposed civil rights legislation, which liberal members of the party celebrated as the defining hallmarks of the Johnson administration.

Johnson, hoping to solidify the party's hold on Illinois, had selected Chicago as the site of the Convention in 1967. The city was solidly Democrat, thanks to a political machine run by Mayor Richard J. Daley. An Irish-American master of political influence, Daley built the Chicago machine into an unassailable structure of favoritism and graft, which—despite a high level of corruption—generally kept order, delivered city services, and facilitated major construction projects like O'Hare Airport, which became the world's busiest in 1963. Daley's firm grip gave him a significant amount of influence in the state Democratic Party as well as with other big-city mayors.

Concerned that antiwar protest might touch off a reprise of the riots that followed the assassination of Martin Luther King Jr., the Daley administration prepared for the worst. Police leave was cancelled, and officers were put on twelve-hour shifts. To bolster the police, units of the Illinois National Guard received training in anti-riot tactics and deployed to Chicago. Daley wanted them on hand so that they could go into action immediately to quell any disturbances.

After a year of assassinations and urban unrest, the International Amphitheatre was put under tight security. The city erected a 2,136-foot-long barbed-wire fence, tarred shut every manhole cover, and installed special machines to check every delegate's credentials. Aircraft were banned in the amphitheatre airspace, roadblocks were constructed, and the sides of the road leading from the downtown Loop to the site of the Convention were walled with plywood. Altogether, the armed security force numbered approximately forty thousand men.[8]

Fight over Credentials

Anticipating conflict over issues of race, the Democratic Party credentialing committee, which made key decisions about which delegates secured the ability to vote in the Convention, attempted to forge a series of compromises between competing delegations from several southern states. These disputes had their roots in the conflict over the **Mississippi Freedom Democratic Party (MFDP)** that had marred the 1964 Convention.

In 1963, although Black people made up 40 percent of the population of Mississippi, the official state delegation to the Democratic National Convention was all white. Frustrated by the obvious racism of their exclusion from the delegation and by a lifetime of oppression, intimidation, and fraud, a group of civil rights activists from Mississippi led by Fannie Lou Hamer, Ella Baker, and Robert Moses held their own elections. Nearly eighty thousand cast "freedom ballots" for an integrated slate of candidates. In 1964, these candidates travelled to the Convention under the banner of the Mississippi Freedom

The **Mississippi Freedom Democratic Party (MFDP)** or the Freedom Democratic Party was created to challenge the authority of the all-white Mississippi delegation to the 1964 Democratic National Convention.

Democratic Party. Under Hamer's leadership, the delegation challenged the right of Mississippi's all-white delegation to participate in the Convention, claiming that they had been illegally elected in a completely segregated process that violated both party regulations and federal law. Hamer's delegation asked to be seated in their stead.

Behind the scenes, all-white delegations from other southern states threatened to bolt from the party if the MFDP were seated. With the help of Vice President Humphrey and Walter Mondale, Johnson crafted a compromise in which the MFDP was offered two non-voting at-large seats; the MFDP refused and denounced the offer as unjust. Hamer explained, "We didn't come all this way for no two seats, 'cause all of us is tired." Many civil rights movement activists felt betrayed by the so-called compromise. Instead of honoring their sacrifices and respecting their advocacy for voting rights, the party sacrificed them for the political interests of white politicians.

Since then, due to the passage of the Voting Rights Act of 1965, the number of Black voters in the South grew dramatically. This encouraged the party to take a stand against all-white delegations. As part of the preparations for the 1968 convention, the party's credentialing committee held a series of contentious meetings, which where chaired by New Jersey governor Richard J. Hughes. This time, the committee insisted upon broad representation from state party organizations. When an all-white delegation arrived from Mississippi, the committee forced them to include Black delegates. When two delegations—one composed entirely of white party stalwarts, the other an integrated collection of McCarthy supporters including Julian Bond—arrived from Georgia, the committee seated half of each. The committee took a particularly determined stand when they refused to seat Georgia governor Lester Maddox, an outspoken and violent racist, in spite of the risk that he would defect to George Wallace's American Independent Party.

Prelude of Violence

Although the city refused to issue permits for protests, most of the demonstrators decided to gather and sleep in Lincoln Park near the Chicago Loop. As Mobe marshals trained protesters in nonviolent resistance, the Yippies began to test the Chicago police. On Friday, August 23, at the Civic Center Plaza, Yippies nominated Pigasus the pig as their presidential candidate. Seven were arrested for creating a public nuisance and the pig was taken into custody.

Subsequently, many of the protest leaders—who had started discussing their options in March—began meeting in an attempt to develop a common strategy, but they disagreed about methods as well as objectives. While the Yippies were focused on holding their Festival of Life, members of the SDS wanted to bring chaos to Chicago's downtown with "disruptive activities." These included stopping traffic, starting trash fires, and breaking windows; the SDS also

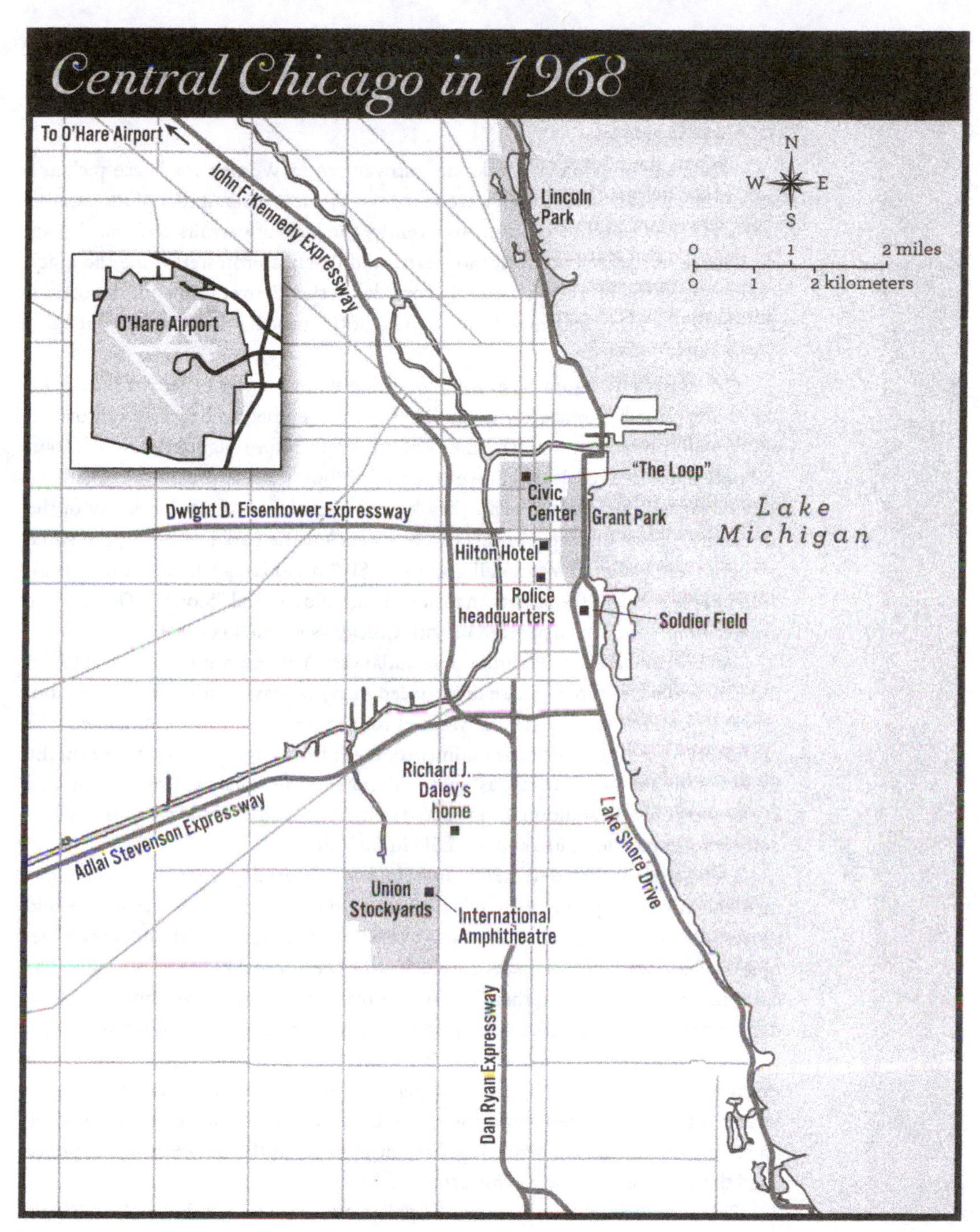

Information for this map was drawn from Adam Conen and Elizabeth Taylor, *American Pharaoh: Mayor Richard J. Daley, His Battle for Chicago and the Nation* (Little Brown & Co., 2000), vi, and Daniel Walker, *Rights in Conflict: Convention Week in Chicago, August 25–29, 1968* (E. P. Dutton & Co., 1968), xii.

encouraged improvisation. The Mobe's David Dellinger succeeded in focusing their thoughts—at least for a while—when he announced that he planned to lead a nonviolent march to the International Amphitheatre once the Convention was in session.

When the nonviolent, moderate antiwar group Women for Peace picketed one of the delegate hotels, they were surprised by the small number of their members who showed up to protest. Apparently, the lack of permits and the threats of violence had scared off most moderate, middle-class protesters. Like the Black freedom movement, they apparently considered the Convention an inopportune moment. The SDS condemned the absence of the moderates: "Our 'liberal base' has finked out big."[9]

On Saturday, August 24, as more out-of-town protesters began arriving, Lincoln Park remained relatively quiet. There often seemed to be more uniformed police than protesters. Many of the protesters left before nightfall, but at 11 PM, the police decided to clear the five hundred to one thousand who remained. As they advanced through the park, they kicked over the bonfires that many of the protesters had set to keep warm. The protesters left the park peacefully, but some of them were gathered into small groups by SDS organizers who led several hundred people through the streets chanting "Peace Now!" and "Stop the Democratic Convention!" They soon blended in with Chicago's weekend crowd.[10]

When combined with rumor and outlandish Yippie promises to put LSD in the Chicago water supply, these protests led many to fear what was to come. Conservative columnist Jack Mabley warned his readers that they could expect the protesters to engage in a wide-ranging program of sabotage, including nails on the freeways, dynamited natural-gas lines, attempts to infiltrate the Convention, and even mortar fire. In addition, he expected that "Yippie girls would work as hookers and try to attract delegates and put LSD in their drinks."[11]

Delegates continued to arrive, and Sunday, August 25, began without serious incident. After the previous night's action, the mood in the park was festive and tense. Allen Ginsberg, a poet who was interested in Eastern mysticism, taught people to chant *om*, which Hindus consider to be the supreme mantra. He hoped to calm the crowd by having them intone the original sound of the universe. Mobe demonstrators left the park to picket several Convention hotels without serious incident. Detroit's MC5, one of the few bands that actually showed up for the Yippie Festival of Life, played for hours, but when the police refused to allow them to play from the back of a flatbed truck, the crowd became angry. They wanted to see the band, and they began to chant, "Pigs eat shit! Pigs eat shit!"[12] In response, the police used their batons and made some arrests.

Tension was high as a new shift of police officers came on duty. When Yippie leader Abbie Hoffman declared the music festival over, five thousand people were in the park, and they were not sure what to do. As night fell, protesters built bonfires and shared drugs. The police periodically rushed in to stomp out the bonfires.

Protest leaders continued to debate strategy. Many members of the SDS wanted to disperse small groups into the city to cause trouble. Others wanted to remain in the park in order to test the curfew.

At around 9 PM, the police decided to form a skirmish line around the park bathrooms. This angered the crowd; they began chanting and throwing stones. In response, the police charged them with their batons several times. In an effort to de-escalate the situation, Mobe marshals encouraged everyone to leave the park. Their efforts convinced some, but not all. Groups shouted, *Revolt! Revolt!*[13]

At 11 PM, the police formed a skirmish line and fired tear gas to push the protesters out of the park. Determined to remain, the protesters retreated to an adjacent parking lot and began shouting, *Hell no, we won't go!* Suddenly, the police moved forward. Their skirmish line dissolved as small groups of officers—many of whom had removed their badges and nameplates—broke ranks to club protesters with their batons. Some were beaten bloody.[14]

Police commanders repeatedly reformed the line, but small groups of officers continued to charge protesters in response to taunts as well as thrown rocks and bottles. Reporters—particularly photographers—were also clubbed by the police. Mobe medics—who were dressed in white—were also beaten. Finally, the large group of protesters dissolved. A few small groups came together and marched toward the Loop chanting *Ho, Ho,* ***Ho Chi Minh****,* but they soon broke apart again. The streets were not cleared until 2 AM.

Ho Chi Minh was the political leader of communist North Vietnam.

The next day, protesters decided to surround the statue of Civil War general John Logan in Grant Park. About one thousand individuals surrounded the statue and raised Vietcong flags. Within ten minutes, the police drove them off with their batons. Afterwards, protesters once again gathered in Lincoln Park, where they continued to debate strategy. Over the course of the day, roaming groups periodically left the park in order to make trouble in the surrounding neighborhood. Some of those who remained in the park, anticipating another clash with the police, began building a barricade.

Ten miles to the south, at the International Amphitheatre, Mayor Daley officially opened the Chicago Democratic Convention. In his opening speech, he declared, "We have no flag burners in this Democratic convention, and I don't think any of them would belong here." Furthermore, he promised, "As long as I am mayor in this city, there's going to be law and order in Chicago."

As a supplement to this essay, you might want to watch the first twenty minutes of "Chicago 1968" a documentary from the PBS *American Experience* series.[15] You may also want to consult David Farber's excellent history, *Chicago '68* (University of Chicago Press, 1994).

PART 3: THE GAME

MAJOR ISSUES FOR DEBATE

During the course of the Convention, delegates must vote to set the party's positions on domestic policy and Vietnam. They must also nominate the Democratic candidate for the presidency. In each case, the delegates must decide with a vote of at least 50% +1 vote. Otherwise, the Convention fails. Protesters and journalists are interested in these questions too, but most of their ability to influence the vote is indirect.

Some delegates may be tempted to determine the outcomes of these votes through caucusing and making backroom deals. While this can create an image of party unity, delegates—particularly the party leaders—should maximize the opportunity for political theater presented by the speeches and press conferences. In the eyes of many voters, open disagreement is acceptable (and even desirable) as long as it eventually evolves into some sort of statesmanlike compromise.

While the delegates attend to the business of the Democratic Party, protesters must decide what they intend to do in order to disrupt the proceedings. A variety of different approaches to protest are available—and each becomes more powerful if it is supported by a large number of protesters.

Domestic Policy

Delegates must choose two domestic policy initiatives to emphasize in the party platform. As the party of Roosevelt's New Deal and Johnson's Great Society, most Democrats support the expansion of the welfare state. However, the civil rights movement, counterculture, urban riots, and the rising cost of the war in Vietnam have made the debate over domestic initiatives divisive. Conservative Democrats, particularly those in the South, now oppose many of Johnson's efforts to expand federal programs. Yet the party will founder unless it moves forward on some domestic programs.

Before the end of **Part 3** of the game, Convention chair Carl Albert must call for a vote to **select two** of the following choices to highlight in the party's domestic platform. Multiple ballots may need to be taken in order to reach a 50% +1 majority for each element. They may not be artfully blended. They must remain distinct.

TIP

Be attentive to the specifics of each policy initiative. Some allow for more local autonomy. Some benefit particular constituencies.

CIVIL RIGHTS	INFRASTRUCTURE	WAR ON POVERTY	LAW AND ORDER
Affirmative action goals and timetables	Increased spending on highways, airports, and railroads	Increased spending on Food Stamps	Increased spending on criminal justice

Civil Rights. This policy plank seeks to challenge discrimination by calling on the federal government to investigate job discrimination in private industry. If discrimination is discovered, the federal government will impose affirmative action hiring goals. Opponents see this as an overreach of federal power.

Background: The Civil Rights Act of 1964 forbade discrimination on the basis of race, religion, sex, or national origin. Intended to integrate public facilities like schools, hospitals, libraries, parks, and swimming pools, it also sought to integrate private businesses that sold to the public, such as motels, restaurants, theaters, and gas stations. Title VII of the Act forbade employers with more than fifteen employees from discriminating in hiring. It also created an enforcement mechanism by establishing the Equal Employment Opportunity Commission (EEOC). Despite these efforts, job discrimination persists; consequently, many Democrats have called for the EEOC to target industries that continue to be discriminatory. They want the EEOC to create goals and timetables to achieve greater integration in their workforces.

Civil rights continues to be a divisive subject in the United States. In September 1966, the Gallup Poll asked, "Do you think the Administration is pushing integration too fast, or not fast enough?" Of the respondents, 52 percent said "too fast." 29 percent thought it was "about right," and only 10 percent said, "not fast enough." In contrast, 51 percent of respondents who did not identify as white thought the pace was "about right," while 32 percent thought it was "not fast enough."[16]

Infrastructure. This policy plank calls for tens of millions of additional federal dollars to construct a variety of projects all over the United States. State and municipal governments will manage these projects. Opponents are concerned about the location of these projects and the potential for graft and corruption.

Background: Since Eisenhower's Federal-Aid Highway Act of 1956, the federal government has lavished aid on a variety of infrastructure projects. This sort of spending is perennially popular because of the jobs it creates and the airports, bridges, and highways that are constructed. The latter are particularly popular with the middle class because they facilitate moving to the suburbs and away from the central cities.

Increased federal spending on infrastructure might encourage the healing of rifts in the party opened by the fights over civil rights. These laws usually involved the distribution of funds from the federal government to state and municipal authorities. These local politicians then made key decisions about the allocation of funds and hiring of contractors. This allowed ample opportunities for low-level corruption. Although this strategy is wasteful, it is also useful for building support for the party and for individual officeholders, and it is popular. In January 1967, when the Gallup Poll asked Americans what they thought about the distribution of federal funds to state and local governments to spend as they saw fit, 70 percent of respondents favored the idea.[17]

Despite these fine qualities, the placement of these projects is increasingly contentious because they tend to be sited in areas with poor and minority populations. Consequently, a number of recent urban interstate projects have been obstructed by citizen activists who resent the idea of large highways plunging through their neighborhoods.

War on Poverty. This policy plank calls for tens of millions of additional dollars to expand the Food Stamp program to millions of impoverished Americans. Opponents are concerned that funding this program may necessitate higher taxes. Others are concerned that it will undermine the work ethic of recipients.

Background: Part of President Johnson's Great Society programs, the Food Stamp Act of 1964, like Medicaid, Head Start, and Job Corps, was overwhelmingly supported by Democrats when it passed into law. Enrollment in the Food Stamps program grew rapidly from half a million in 1965 to two million in 1967. Combined with an increase in agricultural price supports, it sought to connect impoverished Americans to the enormous agricultural bounty of American farms by providing them with coupons redeemable for groceries to supplement other welfare payments. Popular among advocates for the impoverished, Food Stamps are also supported by farmers.

Law and Order. As the historical introduction notes, the assassination of Martin Luther King Jr. sparked riots that erupted across the nation in the summer of 1968. Following this unprecedented series of disturbances, some Democrats think the party should follow the lead of Republican presidential candidate Richard Nixon by promising to spend more money on law enforcement. This policy plank calls for tens of millions of additional dollars for criminal courts, local police, criminal rehabilitation, and the FBI.

Background: Urban riots and fears about the increasing use of illegal drugs have convinced many Americans that their nation is spiraling into chaos. Richard Nixon addressed these concerns in his acceptance speech at the Republican National Convention by promising to be tough on crime. His position resonated with the results of a March 1968 Gallup Poll that asked Americans to comment on the sentencing of convicted criminals by the courts; 63 percent of respondents replied that they were not punished harshly enough. In the wake of last summer's riots, this sentiment is likely to be stronger.[18]

Vietnam Policy

The groundwork for the war in Vietnam was laid by the John F. Kennedy administration, but American involvement in the conflict grew exponentially under his successor, the current president, Lyndon B. Johnson. In an effort to crush the Communist insurgency in South Vietnam, he massively escalated the war by increasing the number of American military personnel in Vietnam from 24,000 when he took office to the current force level of over half a million.

Johnson's escalation also expanded the geographical scope of the war. The United States has been bombing North Vietnam since 1965 in an attempt to halt the flow of supplies from North Vietnam to Communist insurgents in the South, destroy war industries in the North, and force the North into negotiations. Thus far, the United States has dropped more bombs in Vietnam than it did in the entire Pacific theater of WWII. The United States has also become involved in the conflict in neighboring Laos.

Despite these efforts, the conflict drags on and casualties are mounting. In January, hopes that the war was drawing to a close were shattered when the Vietnamese Communists launched the Tet offensive—a series of coordinated assaults on U.S. and South Vietnamese positions throughout South Vietnam. Although they suffered massive casualties, and have lost almost all of their gains in territory, the ability of the Communists to coordinate actions across South Vietnam has convinced many that the war is a stalemate.

Consequently, after his poor showing against peace candidate Senator Eugene McCarthy in the March New Hampshire primary, Johnson unilaterally de-escalated the air war by prohibiting bombing north of the 19th parallel. This meant that Hanoi, the North Vietnamese capital, and the strategically important port of Haiphong are no longer under attack.

This de-escalation may have contributed to the agreement of the North Vietnamese government to begin peace negotiations in Paris in May. Unfortunately, these talks are at an impasse because the North insists upon an end to *all* bombing of North Vietnam and the removal of foreign troops from the South. At present, Johnson is unwilling to accept either of these conditions.

Do You Think the United States Made a Mistake Sending Troops to the Fight in Vietnam?

DATE	% NO
Aug. 1965	61
Mar. 1966	59
May 1966	49
Sep. 1966	48
Nov. 1966	51
Feb. 1967	52
May 1967	50
July 1967	48
Oct. 1967	44
Dec. 1967	46
Feb. 1968	42
Mar. 1968	41
Apr. 1968	40
Aug. 1968	35

Declining Public Support for the War. Support for the war in Vietnam is ebbing. Consider the trajectory of respondents to the following question: *In view of developments since we entered the fighting in Vietnam, do you think the United States made a mistake sending troops to fight in Vietnam?*[19]

In November 1965, soon after the United States started escalating its role in the war, a strong majority of respondents to a Gallup Poll supported U.S. involvement in the war, while only 21 percent disapproved. Most of those polled anticipated that the war would lead to a Korea-style stalemate or U.S. victory. Few thought that the war would drag on. Only a statistically insignificant number expected communist victory.[20]

After the passage of several bloody and largely inconclusive years, support slipped, and in 1968, the idea that the United States had made a mistake by getting involved in the war rapidly gathered support. Despite this, most Americans did not think that the United States was actually losing the war. A poll in June showed that Americans, regardless of whether they considered it a mistake or not, did not consider the war a losing effort. Only 25 percent thought that the United States was losing the war, whereas 47 percent saw the situation as a stalemate. Still, only 18 percent thought that the United States and its allies were making progress.[21]

When contemplating an exit from the war, Americans were clearly divided about which of the frontrunners for the presidential campaign offered the best hope. When asked whether they thought Nixon or Humphrey would do a better job ending the war, each of them were supported by 41 percent of respondents—a dead heat. Despite this partisan division, a strong 66 percent of respondents said that they would support whichever candidate turned more of the war effort over to the South Vietnamese in order to draw down the number of U.S. troops. Only 18 percent opposed this approach.[22]

Policy Options for Vietnam. There are initially only three possible positions on Vietnam. Two additional options may be added if a mainstream journalist publishes or broadcasts a story featuring a delegate calling for the addition of "extreme measures" in Vietnam. If this occurs, the *Victory* and *Withdrawal* options become available. If this does not happen, delegates must limit themselves to the middle three options.

Regardless of the number of options, the party must adopt a clear position on Vietnam policy. During **Part 5** of the game, Convention chair Carl Albert must call for a vote on this issue. Multiple ballots may need to be taken in order to reach a 50% +1 majority.

VICTORY	ESCALATE	MAINTAIN	DE-ESCALATE	*WITHDRAWAL*
No withdrawal from Vietnam can occur until the Communists are defeated	Increase troop levels and resume bombing north of the 19th parallel in an effort to force concessions in Paris	Maintain current troop levels and bombing restrictions	Decrease troop levels and completely halt the bombing of North Vietnam in an effort to break the deadlock in Paris	*Begin total withdrawal of U.S. forces from Vietnam*

Presidential Nomination

The party must nominate Hubert Humphrey, Eugene McCarthy, or George McGovern for president. If a mainstream journalist publishes or broadcasts an interview in which Edward "Ted" Kennedy officially decides to enter the race, he becomes a candidate as well. Smaller games may not include McGovern. If that is the case with your game, drop him as a potential nominee.

Regardless of the number of options, the party must select one of the following nominees. During **Part 7** of the game, Convention chair Carl Albert must call for a vote on this issue. Multiple ballots may need to be taken in order to reach a 50% +1 majority.

Candidates for the nomination must run as individuals. They may run with the understanding that upon being nominated, they will select a particular vice presidential running mate, but there is nothing to hold them to this promise.

Candidates must select a running mate from among the delegates before the end of **Part 6** of the game.

HUMPHREY	MCCARTHY	MCGOVERN	*KENNEDY*

RULES AND PROCEDURES

The Pledge of Allegiance

Every session should begin with the delegates pledging allegiance to the flag. Convention chair Carl Albert should bring the flag of the United States or the representation of the flag to each session and lead the delegates in a recitation.

I pledge allegiance
to the Flag
of the United States of America,
and to the Republic
for which it stands,
one Nation
under God,

indivisible,
with liberty and justice for all.

Protesters may follow along or, after the delegates have completed their pledge, they may offer their own version of the pledge. It might be sincere or mocking.

Rules for Delegates

Voting. The procedures that follow are important. They are, in some ways, the heart of the game. Those who master them may be able to manipulate the outcome to their advantage.

Every member of the Democratic National Convention influences at least 100 delegate votes. Initial vote totals are listed on role sheets, but the number of votes controlled by each delegate is subject to change. Positive stories from *mainstream* journalists may yield additional votes for the session in which the story is published or broadcast. Especially active participation on the floor of the Convention may also increase the number of delegates who support particular players.

> **TIP**
>
> Delegates who earn extra votes should collect Vote Bonus Certificates from the GM.

Because delegates speak on the behalf of numerous delegates, they must announce the number of votes they are casting each time they vote (e.g., "I cast 200 votes in favor of the Infrastructure plank on domestic policy."). Votes may be divided (e.g., "I cast 50 votes for McGovern and 150 for Humphrey."). Delegates may abstain from voting all or a portion of the votes they control, but they must announce that they are doing so.

Convention chair Carl Albert administers the voting. He decides the order in which votes are cast, and after voting is over, shares his count with the Convention secretary (the GM) to verify its accuracy before an announcement is made regarding the results. If Albert is absent John Bailey, the party chair, should appoint a temporary chair to oversee votes.

The Convention must be in session in order for delegates to cast their votes. There is no proxy voting.

If no nominee or platform position receives 50% +1 of the delegate votes present, the Convention must re-ballot until the necessary majority is obtained. The GM may allow a time extension for the session, but only if it appears a majority vote can be reached quickly.

Certain protesters possess Vote Bonus Certificates, which they are able to cast when the Convention votes. See the "Protesters" section for details.

> **TIP**
>
> The Podium Rule does not extend to protesters or journalists.

Podium Rule. Any delegate may queue up at the podium, thereby claiming the absolute right to give the next speech. However, Convention chair Carl Albert has the authority to decide the amount of time speakers may remain at the podium for discussion following the end of the speech. Filibusters are not allowed.

The Smoke-Filled Room. Traditionally, party leaders often made important deals out of the public eye. This often required long, late-night discussions fueled by alcohol and nicotine. Hence, this special deal-cutting opportunity is called the "Smoke-Filled Room." Once per session, John Bailey, chair of the Democratic National Committee, may employ this special power. The Smoke-Filled Room can be a useful way to find a compromise on divisive issues. This puts the Convention into recess, so no votes can be taken while the Smoke-Filled Room is in use. Bailey picks the delegates who will accompany him, but no more than half the delegates may be in the Smoke-Filled Room at any time (round down).

TIP

If Bailey is not in the game, there is no formal Smoke-Filled Room, but players may certainly still have private meetings.

President Johnson. While the president has decided that he will not attend the Convention, he is present in spirit. When the historical delegates arrived in Chicago, they each received a free copy of *To Heal and To Build*, a collection of his speeches. In addition, he has made it known that if necessary, he will join the Convention by landing on the roof of a nearby building in a helicopter. If no clear victor emerges or if the Convention seems hopelessly bogged down, he may decide that he needs to intervene.

If Johnson joins the Convention, Carl Albert, John Bailey, and all potential presidential nominees lose the game because Johnson will have proved them incapable of leading the party in his absence. It is possible that this sort of eleventh-hour intervention is exactly what Johnson wants; it could allow him to act as the savior of the Democratic Party.

Rules for Protesters

The protesters are a mixed bag. Their ideologies and approaches to protest stretch across a wide spectrum, but some observers group them with a collective label: The "New Left." As opposed to the "Old Left" with its focus on Marxism, economics, and working-class politics, the New Left grew out of the white middle class and seeks the transformation of society as a whole. As writer Norman Mailer explains, "The New Left was interested for the most part in altering society (and being conceivably altered themselves—they were nothing if not Romantic) by the activity of working for a new kind of life out in the ghettoes, the campuses, and the antiwar movement."[23]

Many Black civil rights organizations like the SCLC, CORE, and SNCC are conspicuously absent from the protest. Many of the leaders of these organizations saw little to gain from protesting the Democratic Party. In addition, some local Black activists were threatened with preemptive arrest. Consequently, most members of these organizations have opted to stay away, but a few have decided to attend.

New ideologies are also present. Some of the women among the protesters, tired of being treated as second-class citizens, have started developing a feminist consciousness, but they are not organized. There are also poets, musicians, and oddballs of various sorts.

The Protest Zone. Although the game places protesters and delegates in the same classroom, the protesters are in Grant Park, which is miles away from the International Amphitheatre, but quite close to the hotels in which the delegates are staying. To simulate this distance, Mayor Daley will define a Protest Zone within the classroom. (If Daley is absent, the Protest Zone will be defined by Convention chair Carl Albert.) It must include the entire back wall and sufficient seating for all protesters.

Unless they are launching a demonstration, protesters must remain within this Protest Zone. After Part 1, journalists who are not issued press credentials by Mayor Daley must also remain within this Protest Zone (unless they join a demonstration). Credentialed journalists may visit the Protest Zone at any time.

Protester Speeches. Protesters give speeches during Parts 2, 4, and 6 of the game. Depending upon the structure of a particular game session, the GM will occasionally halt the proceedings of the Convention and direct everyone's attention to the Protest Zone. At this point, protesters are allowed to give speeches or make any statements they wish. Protesters should feel free to stand on chairs and tables, signifying their desire to have their voices heard. The Convention is in recess during this part of the session. Once the protesters have finished their speeches and protests, it may reconvene.

Protester Political Influence. Protesters have some influence inside the Convention. Each session's **Media Darling** should receive a Vote Bonus Certificate from the GM. This is the protester who gained the most media attention during the preceding session as determined by the GM. In order to become the Media Darling, attracting the attention of the underground press is more important than attracting mainstream journalists.

The Media Darling for the first session is Abbie Hoffman.

The Protest Leader should also receive a Vote Bonus Certificate from the GM. At the end of each session the protesters in the Protest Zone vote to elect their leader for the following session. Ordinarily, each protester casts a single vote, but there are some exceptions:

- If Bella Abzug is wearing a particularly nice hat, she casts a double vote.
- Fritz Wehrenburg, Vivian Rothstein, and Hillary Rodham all have double votes.

The Protest Leader for the first session is Tom Hayden.

Jail and Hospital. The GM will designate part of the classroom as jail. Protesters and journalists who are jailed may only talk to other prisoners. All prisoners are released at the end of the session. Mayor Daley may order their early release.

The GM shall also designate a hospital for injured protesters and journalists. Patients cannot speak publicly for the rest of the session, but journalists may interview them. The GM determines the speed of their recovery by rolling a die at the end of the session in which they are hospitalized.

WARNING! *Jailed or hospitalized protesters are unable to use Vote Bonus Certificates. They also lose the ability to vote for the next Protest Leader.*

Ordinarily, those who are accidentally *killed* by the police or end up in *intensive care* lose the game. They cannot participate; they may only observe. This should give these players ample time to write a blistering final essay (perhaps from the point of view of a grieving friend or loved one), which they must circulate to journalists at least twenty-four hours before the debriefing session.

Hospitalization Table

DIE ROLL	RESULT
1–4	Full recovery—return to the game
5	Remain in hospital—remain in hospital for the next part of the game
6	Intensive care—no actions for the rest of the game

Apprehend with the Chicago PD. During Parts 2, 4, and 6 of the game, Mayor Daley may order the police to arrest one protester. If he does so, the GM then rolls a die.

News stories may warn specific protesters that an arrest attempt is planned for a specific session. If this occurs, the target gains a +1 to the die roll.

Apprehension Table

DIE ROLL	RESULT
1–3	The player is placed under arrest and is taken to jail.
4	The oblivious target is not located by the police.
5–6	The target slips through the fingers of plainclothes officers; the GM will inform the target that the police attempted an arrest.

If the arrest attempt is successful, Daley may opt to have this player *beaten down* while in custody. This will send the prisoner to the hospital.

Protests and Crackdowns. Protests may only be mounted during Parts 2, 4, and 6 of the game. Several forms of demonstration are available to the protesters. Each option ratchets up the level of unrest. This, in turn, probably ensures increased press coverage. It also increases the potential for violent action by the Chicago Police Department, which is controlled by Mayor Daley (and in his absence by Carl Albert).

In order to stage a **sit-in** or **riot**, at least one journalist must release a news story for the appropriate session that includes quotations from at least one protester calling for a demonstration. The story must identify a specific form of protest. Protesters may stage a **march** without an accompanying news story.

NOTE

If you are playing a version of the game without journalists, ignore this requirement.

Before leaving the Protest Zone, protesters must decide on the form of protest they intend to stage. If there is disagreement, the form of the protest is determined by the Protest Leader.

During a demonstration, protesters leave the Protest Zone together. Journalists may accompany them. Cautious protesters and uncredentialed journalists may decide to remain in the Protest Zone where there is less risk of arrest, but they should recognize that they still are at the mercy of Mayor Daley if a demonstration is launched.

The first kind of demonstration is a **march**. This action is nonviolent and does not require a news story to launch. When the action begins, the Protest Leader announces that the protesters are marching on the Convention site. They then leave the Protest Zone and circle the classroom, chanting slogans. They must stay together and they must keep marching. After the protesters have circled the room one time, Daley may order the Chicago Police to arrest them and send them to jail. If the police fail to arrest all of the demonstrators, the protesters who escaped arrest may return to the Protest Zone or circle the room a second time. There is then a *second* chance for the police to arrest the demonstrators. If any protesters escape the second arrest attempt, the demonstration is a success and they return to the Protest Zone.

TIP

Protest organizers may recruit people who are not playing the game in an effort to stage a truly impressive demonstration. Large numbers of protesters can also help to confuse the police.

The second kind of demonstration is a **sit-in**. This action is nonviolent and requires a news story to launch. When the action begins, the Protest Leader announces that the protesters are staging a sit-in to disrupt the Convention. They then leave the Protest Zone and circle the classroom, chanting slogans. They must stay together and they must keep marching. After the protesters have circled the room one time, the Chicago Police may attempt to arrest them and send them to jail. If the police fail to arrest all of the demonstrators, any protesters who escaped arrest may peacefully occupy the podium, temporarily disrupting the proceedings of the Convention. If this occurs, the sit-in is a success! There is then a *second* chance for the police to arrest the demonstrators. Protesters who escape the second arrest attempt return to the Protest Zone.

The third kind of demonstration is a **riot**. In order to stage a riot, protesters must have staged a successful march or sit-in during an earlier game session. A *riot* requires a news story to launch. When the action begins, the Protest Leader announces that the protesters are starting a riot in order to disrupt the Convention. They then leave the Protest Zone and circle the classroom chanting *aggressive and profane* slogans. They must stay together and they must keep marching. After the protesters have circled the room one time, the Chicago Police may attempt to arrest them and send them to jail. If the police fail to arrest all of the demonstrators, all hell breaks loose in the streets of Chicago. This means the riot is a success! There is then a second chance to arrest the demonstrators. If the streets are not cleared with the second attempt, the Convention is suspended for the rest of the session and any scheduled Convention votes are delayed, or perhaps even cancelled, as a result.

WARNING! *There may be two different police actions against protesters during each session.*

Mass Arrests and Beatings. The GM conducts arrested protesters and journalists to jail. Protesters who are *beaten down* must go to the hospital.

Rules for Journalists

Unlike delegates or protesters, journalists do not give speeches, vote, or lead protests. Instead, they report on these events. **Mainstream** journalists work for a variety of generally respected institutions like the *Washington Post*, *Newsweek*, the *New York Times*, and CBS News. Consequently, their stories have an impact on the proceedings of the Convention and, ultimately, in the general elections in November. **Underground journalists** are more tuned in to the counterculture, so the impact of their work is strongest among the protesters, but they have an impact on November as well.

Power of the Press. Delegates and protesters seek the attention of journalists because they amplify their words and gain the power to affect public opinion. Almost all of the players want to talk to journalists, and only a few want to keep their plans hidden. Many of the benefits of being featured in stories written by journalists are indirect, but for purposes of the game, there are direct benefits as well.

Stories that are distributed by mainstream journalists during the game have the following effects:

- If the stories are positive, Delegates who are featured most prominently in the stories gain Vote Bonus Certificates.

- In games with lots of players, Press Secretaries may earn additional Vote Bonus Certificates for their delegates if mainstream journalists release stories that put their candidates in a positive light.

TIP

Ordinarily, the GM will distribute no more than one Vote Bonus Certificate to each player during each game session.

- Delegates may add additional options for the Vietnam plank if a news story published or broadcast before **Part 5** begins features an influential Dove or a Hawk calling for "Extreme Measures" in Vietnam. If such a position is taken, two new options are added: *Withdrawal* and *Victory*.
- Delegates must air their grievances against the Democratic Party leadership in a news story in order to stage a Walkout from the Convention.
- Delegates with vice presidential ambitions must be featured in a news story in order to join the ticket.
- Edward "Ted" Kennedy must be featured in a news story before he can throw his hat in the ring in pursuit of the presidential nomination.

News stories that are distributed by mainstream or underground journalists have the following effects:

- Protesters featured in news stories may become the Media Darling. In this case, stories by underground journalists are twice as influential as those of mainstream journalists.
- Protesters may not stage sit-ins or riots unless they air their grievances in a news story.
- Protesters in news stories that are identified as targets of the Chicago Police Department are more likely to elude capture by plainclothes officers who attempt to apprehend them.

TIP

If you are a protester profiled by a journalist, take a copy of the story to the GM to improve your chances of becoming the Media Darling.

Convention Access. Press access to the Convention has been strictly limited by Mayor Daley. All journalists have access for Part 1 of the game, but in later sessions Daley may suspend their credentials, banning them from the Convention. Journalists without press credentials must go to the Protest Zone.

Journalistic Ethics. If mainstream journalists hear rumors, they are hearsay, which must be substantiated before they can be published. The first step should be to contact the subject of the rumor for comment.

Example: If Tom Wicker gets a tip that Ted Kennedy intends to run for the presidential nomination, he must attempt to reach him for a comment.

> If he receives no response to his inquiries, he should report, "Kennedy could not be reached for comment."
>
> If he reaches him, but Kennedy refuses to comment, he should report, "Kennedy refused to comment."
>
> If Kennedy agrees to an interview, he and Wicker should determine ground rules using the section below.

Journalists may speak to anyone, during or outside class sessions. When doing so, they must adhere to basic journalistic principles. Most importantly, they must establish ground rules for interviews. At the outset, they should discuss the terms of the interview with their subject and choose from one of the following:

> On the record means journalists can attribute whatever the subject says by name. For example, "'Nixon is a fascist,' said Yippie leader Abbie Hoffman."
>
> Off the record means journalists negotiate some kind of attribution acceptable to the subject. For example, after an off-the-record interview with Mayor Daley, a journalist might write, "'McCarthy doesn't have the votes.' said a high-ranking party official knowledgeable about the delegate count at the Convention."
>
> On background means journalists cannot publish anything without substantiation from another source. In that case, journalists would attribute the information to those other sources, not to the source speaking "on background." For example, if Walter Mondale told a journalist on background that Vice President Humphrey had approached Ed Muskie about the possibility of becoming his running mate, the journalist should seek comments from Humphrey and Muskie.

TIP

In essence, speaking "on background" is a way for someone who wants to remain anonymous to drop hints.

If a mainstream journalist violates these rules, the story might be "spiked" by an editor (the GM). This kills the story before publication. Editors might do this in order to protect their publications from libel or slander suits. Underground journalists have fewer restrictions. That is part of what makes them exciting. It also makes them less reliable and more vulnerable to accusations of libel.

Libel and Slander. Journalists must not disseminate demonstrably false statements that are damaging to a person's reputation. This is defamation. Slander refers to doing this with the spoken word, whereas libel refers to doing this in print. Players who believe journalists have slandered or libeled them may bring suit against them. In order to do so, they must write up specific charges, including quotations from appropriate sources, and present them to the GM before the end of the game. If the accusation is sound, the journalist in question loses the game and all journalists working for the same organization lose the ability to win a Pulitzer Prize.

TIP

Mainstream journalists should be particularly cautious about libel and slander. They are held to a higher standard.

Winning Pulitzer Prizes. The events at the upcoming Convention should produce a great deal of good journalism, but some stories will rise above the others. This will make their authors eligible for Pulitzer Prizes. When journalists submit their final stories to the GM, they should also submit the author and title of two pieces by other journalists that they found especially compelling. Up to three prizes may be awarded by the GM.

- The National Reporting Prize
- The Investigative Reporting Prize
- The Editorial Reporting Prize

Objectives and Victory Conditions

Delegates are attempting to get their preferences for domestic policy, Vietnam, and presidential nominee adopted by the party as a whole. In addition, certain delegates shall strive to hold the party together. Some must also promote their personal ambitions to secure a place on the ticket as the presidential or vice presidential nominee.

Protesters are either partisans attempting to shape the demonstrations to fit their particular ideology or young people searching for political consciousness. They are all against the war and in favor of civil rights. Generally, protesters win if they succeed in persuading the delegates to support their ideas by incorporating them into the platform and by challenging the status quo in the nomination process, but some will not be satisfied unless they cause a ruckus.

Journalists are attempting to cover the story. Even though many possess political sympathies, these are not at the forefront of their writing or the ambitions of mainstream journalists. Instead, they are attempting to write stories worthy of the Pulitzer Prize. Underground journalists are often more political. They are also often practitioners of the "New Journalism." Rather than encouraging disinterested observation, this approach places the writer at the center of the story.

The November Election

Almost everyone is interested in the outcome of the general election in November. At the outset of the game, there is an equal chance of Republican or Democratic victory. This balance is altered by the events of the game; the outcome will be determined with the roll of a die. Several factors modify this die roll. Most, but not all, of these factors are listed below.

The Democrats are more likely to win if:

- Most stories published or broadcast by journalists are positive about:
    - The presidential and vice presidential candidates.
    - The positions taken by the party on domestic policy.
    - The positions taken by the party on Vietnam.
    - The management of the Convention itself.
- The party engages in "ticket balancing" by making sure that the presidential and vice presidential candidates are from different regions of the United States.
- There are no walkouts.
- No more than one demonstration is successful.
- There is no excessive violence in the streets.

They are more likely to do poorly if the opposite occurs.

TIP

Mainstream journalists have greater influence upon American voters than underground journalists.

BASIC OUTLINE OF THE GAME

Parts and Sessions. Before the game begins, most instructors will conduct at least one setup session. This orients players to the historical context for the game and allows them to begin to interact with one another in role. After the game ends, most instructors help players reflect upon the experience, share secrets, and determine victors. Between these bookends, the instructor becomes the Gamemaster and oversees the operation of the game.

To allow the game to work in a wide variety of formats, it is subdivided into seven parts, which individual instructors may combine into sessions of varying lengths. All assignments are tied to specific parts, so check with your instructor to see how the parts are arranged for your game.

Setup Session: Background and Context

Individual instructors can use this session to integrate the game into the themes of their particular courses. Instructors should distribute role sheets *before* this class, and they should allow players some time to interact in role.

TIP

In conjunction with the setup session, some instructors will assign a short quiz about the historical context essay.

Delegates should use this time to talk with their allies and perhaps some of the undecided delegates. Protesters should have a "**rap session**," allowing everyone's voice to be heard. Journalists should use this time to talk to delegates and protesters. Some of them have stories due at the very beginning of the game. They may use this opportunity to set up interviews. Similarly, some delegates and protesters may want to seek out journalists so that they can use the Power of the Press to advance their agendas.

A rap session is an informal, non-hierarchical conversation about an important subject.

Throughout the Convention

Carl Albert is not ordinarily required to present a formal speech because he is responsible for maintaining order and decorum in the chamber. He is also responsible for counting votes as well as setting the agenda and keeping it moving along. To this end, he shall:

- Lead the Pledge of Allegiance at the beginning of each session.
- Organize the order of speakers for each session.
- Accommodate questions from journalists and from the delegates.

BEFORE THE FIRST GAME SESSION

Journalists release their stories. The journalists who are scheduled to publish stories during the first session will need to write them before the game begins in earnest. They should draw heavily upon the Historical Background and the Core Texts in this game book, but they may also attempt to arrange interviews with other players.

If delegates or protesters agree to interviews before the game begins, it will advance their objectives. Delegates may receive a Vote Bonus Certificate. If protesters want to stage a sit-in during Part 2, they must get a journalist to publish or broadcast a story with a call for it.

The GM will coordinate with these journalists to distribute their stories to other players. These arrangements may allow players to read these stories before Part 1 begins. Check with your GM for details. Most of the stories for Part 1 are from mainstream journalists, and, depending on role assignments in your class, may include:

> **Tom Wicker** will publish a liberal opinion column in the *New York Times*.
>
> **Walter Trohan** will publish a conservative opinion column in the *Chicago Tribune*.
>
> **Mike Royko** will publish an opinion column well-grounded in Chicago lore in the Chicago *Daily News*.

GAME BEGINS

PART 1: WELCOME AND DEBATE ON DOMESTIC POLICY

Room setup. Delegates want to be able to hear the speeches of other delegates, so they should sit near the front of the room. Mayor Daley, assisted by the GM, should conduct protesters to the Protest Zone. Initially, all journalists have access to the Convention, so they may sit where they like. The GM should indicate the location of the jail and hospital in case players need to go there at some point in the game.

The Convention begins. After players have an opportunity to read stories by journalists, Convention chair **Carl Albert** will lead the delegates in the recitation of the Pledge of Allegiance. Protesters may accompany them. Alternatively, they may recite their own version of the Pledge. Afterward, protesters may boo or cheer, but they must allow the delegates to carry on with their business.

To open the Convention, Mayor **Richard J. Daley** will give a speech welcoming the delegates to the great city of Chicago. Several delegates will then give speeches advocating for different domestic policy priorities. The number of speeches depends upon the number of players in your version of the game and may include:

Representative **Julian Bond** of Georgia will speak in favor of Civil Rights and the War on Poverty.

Senator **Fred Harris** of Oklahoma will speak in favor of Infrastructure and the War on Poverty.

Representative **Hale Boggs** of Louisiana will speak in favor of Infrastructure and the War on Poverty.

Convention voting. In the unlikely event that Carl Albert calls for a vote, the Protest Leader and Media Darling may cast their votes along with the delegates.

PART 2: FIRST PROTEST

After the delegates finish their speeches and answer any questions, the action shifts to the Protest Zone. Delegates may want to pay attention to the protesters, but they may prefer to spend this time caucusing with the other delegates or talking to journalists. Protesters may find this annoying and disrespectful. If this results in too much real-world frustration, GMs may require delegates to pay attention to the protesters. Speeches by protesters may include:

Abbie Hoffman of the Yippies will nominate Pigasus, a pig, for president.

Tom Hayden of Students for a Democratic Society (SDS) will give a speech grounded in the ideas of the Port Huron Statement.

Allen Ginsberg will read poetry.

Bobby Seale of the Black Panthers will speak on the Black Panther Ten Point program.

Apprehension. During these speeches, Mayor Daley may order the police (the GM) to apprehend one of the protesters. If Daley makes this decision, the GM takes appropriate action. Protesters apprehended in the middle of a speech may not finish. If apprehended before they have a chance to give a scheduled speech, they must wait to give it in Part 4. The GM will conduct arrested protesters to jail.

Demonstration. Any protester may call for a march. If one of the journalists published a story for Part 1 that included a call for a sit-in, protesters may do that instead. If there is disagreement regarding the form that the demonstration should take, the Protest Leader makes the choice. During Part 1, that is Tom Hayden.

Police crackdown. During the demonstration, Mayor Daley (or, in his absence, Carl Albert) may deploy the police to arrest protesters as well as any journalists who are not in the Convention Hall. If this occurs, the GM identifies protesters who get arrested or beaten down by the police. Any remaining protesters must then decide if they want to return to the Protest Zone. If they decide to continue the demonstration, the police may move in a second time, in which case the GM will once again make arrests. If any protesters remain after a second police action, the demonstration is a success.

Protest Leader and Media Darling selection. After the demonstration ends, all protesters who are not in jail or the hospital may elect the next Protest Leader. Some have double votes. The GM names the next Media Darling by assessing all of the pieces published by journalists. The GM will provide them with Vote Bonus Certificates.

Jail and hospital. At the very end of Part 2, any protesters who are in jail may leave. The GM will determine the status of protesters who are in the hospital by rolling a die. Protesters who go into intensive care at this point may decide to begin playing new roles.

PART 3: KEYNOTE AND DOMESTIC POLICY VOTE

After the protest ends, the next portion of the Convention begins. Note that this may occur during the same class session. Different GMs arrange the parts in different ways to accommodate a variety of class sizes and times.

Dan Rather of CBS news will begin this part of the game with a stand-up interview. This may have been recorded and edited beforehand, in which case the GM will arrange for a screening. Alternatively, it may be live. In that case, everyone directs their attention to Rather and his interviewee.

Paul Krassner, an underground journalist who writes for *The Realist,* will publish a piece about the Convention. The humor may be crude.

If this is the beginning of a new session, Carl Albert will lead the delegates in the Pledge of Allegiance. Unlike in Part 1, when all journalists had access to the Convention Hall, Mayor Daley may now decide to exclude certain journalists. If Daley denies access, they must go to the Protest Zone. Possible speeches include:

Senator **Daniel Inouye** of Hawaii will present a keynote address that will emphasize the unity of the Democratic Party. This may earn him a Vote Bonus Certificate.

Senator **Robert Byrd** of West Virginia will speak in favor of Law and Order.

Vice President **Hubert Humphrey** will remind everyone of the great accomplishments of President Lyndon B. Johnson's administration.

Mr. **John M. Bailey** of Connecticut, the chair of the National Democratic Party, will attempt to focus delegates on defeating Richard Nixon and George Wallace.

Walkouts? If a story published or broadcast by a mainstream journalist includes a call for a walkout by Hawks, Doves, or civil rights activists, those players should leave the Convention before voting begins. They may return after voting ends.

The delegates vote to determine domestic priorities. Carl Albert must construct the voting on this issue with care so that the delegates determine two domestic policy priorities for the party platform by a 50% +1 margin. They must choose from four possibilities: Civil Rights, the War on Poverty, Infrastructure, and Law and Order. He may decide to have multiple ballots with each eliminating the lowest priority. Alternatively, he may decide to have two votes, each of which requires delegates to choose between two priorities. The current Protest Leader and Media Darling may cast their votes along with the delegates.

PART 4: SECOND PROTEST

Journalists release interviews. The stories for this part of the game are all interviews, but they take a variety of forms. These journalists should work with the GM in order to make them available to other players. If the stories are available before the class meets, other players should endeavor to access them. Possibilities include:

Hal Bruno will publish an interview in *Newsweek.*

Aline Saarinen of NBC will broadcast a live or recorded interview in the same manner as Dan Rather in Part 3.

Haynes Johnson of the *Washington Star* and NBC will either publish an interview or broadcast it. It is the player's choice.

Hunter S. Thompson and **William S. Burroughs**, who are working on longer pieces, must submit their notes to their editors (the GM).

After players have an opportunity to read, watch, or hear these stories, the action shifts to the Protest Zone. Once again, delegates may or may not pay attention. If any protesters were unable to give their speeches because the police arrested them in Part 2, they may do so now. Possibilities include:

David Dellinger of the Mobe will speak about nonviolent protest.

Bella Abzug of the Women's Strike Organization will condemn the war in Vietnam.

Dick Gregory, the comedian, will speak about nonviolent protest, the civil rights movement, and his candidacy for the presidency.

Allen Ginsberg will read more poetry.

Jerry Rubin will denounce the Chicago police department and will call for an end to the war in Vietnam. *Yippie!*

Apprehension. Once again, during these speeches, Mayor Daley may order the police (the GM) to apprehend one of the protesters. As was the case in Part 2, any arrest is immediate. The GM will conduct arrested protesters to jail.

Demonstration. Any protester may call for a march. If one of the journalists published a story including a call for a sit-in, protesters may do that instead. If the first demonstration was a success, and there is a story featuring a protester calling for a riot, they may also decide to do that. If there is disagreement regarding the form that the demonstration should take, the Protest Leader makes the choice.

Police crackdown. During the demonstration, Mayor Daley (or, in his absence, Carl Albert) may deploy the police to arrest protesters as well as any journalists who are not in the Convention Hall. If this occurs, the GM identifies any protesters arrested or beaten down by the police. Any remaining protesters must then decide if they want to return to the Protest Zone. If they decide to continue the demonstration, the police may move in a second time, in which case the GM will once again make arrests. If any protesters remain after a second police action, the demonstration is a success.

Protest Leader and Media Darling selection. After the demonstration ends, all protesters who are not in jail or the hospital may elect the next Protest Leader. Some protesters have double votes. The GM names the next Media Darling by assessing all of the pieces published by journalists. The GM will provide them with Vote Bonus Certificates.

Jail and hospital. Any protesters who are in jail may leave. The GM will determine the status of protesters who are in the hospital by rolling a die.

PART 5: DEBATE AND VOTE ON VIETNAM

Two important journalists may weigh in at this point. One of them is the voice of authority. Some call him "the most trusted man in America." The other is a wildly irreverent comedian who is likely to offend.

> **Walter Cronkite**, the CBS news anchor, should present a live or recorded television interview.
>
> **Paul Krassner** will publish another piece of satire.

If this is the beginning of a new session, Carl Albert will lead the delegates in the Pledge of Allegiance. Once again, Mayor Daley may decide to exclude certain journalists. He may also decide to readmit journalists who he excluded during Part 3. If Daley denies journalists access, they must go to the Protest Zone.

This part of the game, in which the Democrats will determine the party's position on the Vietnam War, is likely to be tense. Initially, there are three possibilities: Escalation, Maintain, and De-escalation. If a prominent Hawk or Dove is the focus of a story that is broadcast or published before this point, two additional options may become available: Victory and Withdrawal. Albert must announce the range of possible policies before the speeches begin. They may include:

> Senator **Eugene McCarthy** of Minnesota will speak on ending the war.
>
> Governor **John Connally** of Texas will speak in favor of escalating the war.
>
> Mrs. **Fannie Lou Hamer** of Mississippi will denounce the racist war in Vietnam.
>
> Senator **Edward "Ted" Kennedy** of Massachusetts will speak about the stalemate in Vietnam. He will also announce his intentions regarding the race for the presidential nomination if he has not already done so. This may gain him a Vote Bonus Certificate.

Walkouts? If a story published or broadcast by a mainstream journalist includes a call for a walkout by Hawks, Doves, or civil rights activists, those players should leave the Convention before voting begins. They may return after voting ends.

The delegates vote to determine Vietnam policy. Carl Albert should construct the voting on this issue with care in order to make sure that the delegates determine Vietnam policy by a 50% +1 margin. The current Protest Leader and Media Darling may cast their votes along with the delegates.

PART 6: THIRD PROTEST

As the fight for the nomination comes closer, a large number of journalists release their stories. Given the volume of stories for this part of the game, the GM may want to set aside time for players to read, watch, and listen to them. Alternatively, the GM may require players to do this ahead of time. Check with your GM for details.

> **Tom Wicker**, **Walter Trohan**, and **Mike Royko** will all publish their second opinion pieces. (They all published at the beginning of Part 1.)
>
> **Hal Bruno** and **Aline Saarinen** will also publish or broadcast their second pieces, but they have a quicker turnaround; they first published in Part 4.

After players have an opportunity to read, watch, or hear the stories by the journalists, the action shifts to the Protest Zone, where the protesters are likely to react to whatever decision the Democrats made regarding their Vietnam policy. Once again, delegates may or may not pay attention to them. If any protesters were unable to give their speeches because the police arrested them in Part 5, they may do so now. Speeches may include:

> **Vivian Rothstein** of SDS will speak about Vietnam. If police action at the end of Part 4 resulted in injuries, she will share her outrage.
>
> **Kathy Boudin** of SDS will speak about urban poverty unless police action resulted in injuries. In that case, she will be very angry.
>
> **Fritz Wehrenberg**, a student from Valparaiso University, will describe the protester that he finds most inspiring.
>
> **Allen Ginsberg** will recite some poetry.

Apprehension. During these speeches, Mayor Daley may order the police (the GM) to apprehend one of the protesters. If Daley makes this decision, the GM determines the result and takes appropriate action. Unlike earlier parts of the game, protesters apprehended before or in the middle of their speeches may finish, but they may not answer questions afterward. The GM will conduct arrested protesters to jail.

Demonstration. Any protester may call for a march. If one of the journalists who published a story included the call for a sit-in, protesters may do that instead. If a demonstration in Part 2 or 4 was a success (protesters remained after two police actions), and a journalist publishes a story calling for a riot, that becomes an option as well. If there is disagreement regarding the form that the protest should take, the Protest Leader makes the choice.

Police crackdown. During the demonstration, Mayor Daley (or, in his absence, Carl Albert) may deploy the police to arrest protesters as well as any journalists who are not in the Convention Hall. If this occurs, the GM identifies any protesters arrested or beaten down by the police. Any remaining protesters must then decide if they want to return to the Protest Zone. If they decide to continue the demonstration, the police may move in a second time, in which case the GM will once again make arrests. If any protesters remain with the demonstration after a second police action, the demonstration is a success.

Protest Leader and Media Darling selection. After the demonstration ends, all protesters who are not in jail or the hospital may elect the final Protest Leader. Some protesters have double votes. The GM names the final Media Darling by assessing all of the pieces published by journalists. The GM will provide them with Vote Bonus Certificates.

Jail and hospital. Any protesters who are in jail may leave. The GM will determine the status of protesters who are in the hospital by rolling a die.

PART 7: DEBATE AND BALLOTING ON THE PARTY NOMINEE

If this is the beginning of a new session, Carl Albert will lead the delegates in the Pledge of Allegiance. Once again, Mayor Daley may decide to exclude certain journalists. He may also decide to readmit journalists. If Daley denies journalists access, they must go to the Protest Zone.

Both **Walter Cronkite** and **Dan Rather** should conduct interviews at the beginning of this part of the game. These may provide presidential nominees and their supporters with a great chance to launch their battles for the nomination. Following these interviews, delegates will speak about the nominees.

Games with more than thirty-five players may include nominating speeches, but in smaller games, potential nominees must represent themselves. To begin the session, Senator **Edmund "Ed" Muskie** of Maine will review the potential nominees.

TIP

If this part of the game wraps up quickly, the GM may decide to shift into debriefing ahead of time.

Walkouts? If a story published or broadcast by a mainstream journalist includes a call for a walkout by Hawks, Doves, or civil rights activists, those players should leave the Convention before voting begins.

The delegates vote to select the Democratic Party nominee for president. Carl Albert must construct the vote with care to ensure that the delegates elect their nominee for president by a 50% +1 margin. Electing a candidate on the first ballot will strengthen the chances of a victory in November. The current Protest Leader and Media Darling may cast their votes along with the delegates.

After the party selects the nominee, the nominee names his running mate. At this point, the game ends.

DEBRIEFING: ELECTION OF 1968

Reflection. For this session, all players must write a final reflection from the point of view of their roles. The GM may want to distribute these electronically so that people have a chance to read the reflections of other players.

Outcomes. After determining the attitude of journalists toward the Convention, the GM will roll dice and determine the results of the general election in November. The GM will also determine the recipients of Pulitzer Prizes (if any). For some players, these determine victory or defeat. At this point, the game is complete and the GM returns to being an instructor.

TIP

Journalists who are guilty of defamation lose the ability to cast votes for the Pulitzer. Furthermore, no members of their organization are eligible for the prize.

Secrets. Once the instructor announces these decisions, players are free to divulge any secrets that they concealed over the course of the game. This is a good way for them to return to themselves. Players may also want to share the ways in which they resonated with their roles as well as the degree to which their personal beliefs diverge from the roles they inhabited for the course of the game. This may be particularly important for players with roles that were sexist, racist, violent, or extremely irritating.

What really happened? The instructor will outline the historical events surrounding the Chicago Convention. This provides good opportunities for making comparisons and analyzing causation. This discussion may include handouts of historical documents.

What happened next? The instructor will briefly describe the later lives of the different roles.

Victory. Every role has slightly different objectives. In order to determine the victors, your instructor may ask you to write a short self-assessment that incorporates the outcomes that are determined at the beginning of the debriefing session.

ASSIGNMENTS

Delegates and Protesters

Note: Your instructor may change the parameters of the written and spoken assignments for your game. Make sure that you confirm the specifics before the game begins.

Delegates and protesters must all give one 2–3 minute **speech**. The timing and topics for all of these speeches are listed on their role sheets and on the outline above.

Ordinarily, these speeches should be accompanied by 1,000–1,200-word **essays** on the same topic. These should include quotations from *at least three* of the documents in the game book and should be submitted to the GM.

After the game ends, delegates and protesters are all responsible for submitting a 1,000–1,200-word **reflective essay**. These should be written from the point of view of their roles. Topics for these essays vary. Details are included in the role sheets.

Journalists

During the Convention, journalists are required to create stories for publication or broadcast. They are responsible for disseminating their work to other players (by making copies, projecting, or posting electronically). If the logistics of dissemination are difficult, they should discuss various options with the GM.

Mainstream print journalists should follow these guidelines for their stories unless their role sheets give other directions:

1. Place a headline at the top of your story that includes the name of the person that your story focuses upon.
2. Place your byline (your name and organization) below the headline.
3. Single space your copy.
4. Use a two-column format.
5. Use narrow margins.
6. Fit everything on a single page.
7. Include quotations from at least one other player who is not a journalist.
8. Include quotations from at least three documents in the game book.

Mainstream television journalists should follow these guidelines:

1. Begin your broadcast by identifying yourself and your news organization.

2. Identify your location. Are you in the Convention Hall? Outside with the protesters? At your desk?
3. Create short broadcasts. This invariably means that you need to edit your raw footage down to the essentials.
4. Include at least one other player who is not a journalist.
5. Include quotations from at least three documents in the game book.

Underground journalists should follow many of the same rules, but their pieces are longer and more experimental. The various deviations from these norms are described on their role sheets.

TIP

Larger games may include journalists that work with different media, including photography, radio, cartoons, and broadsheets.

Different Sorts of Stories

Journalists may take a number of different approaches when they write their stories.[24]

As it happened: These are summaries of the key events that occurred during the prior game session. They recount the events of the Convention for the general public, who are ordinary Americans. This type of news story is usually assigned to greenhorn journalists because it is simple and does not require many contacts or a lot of investigative work.

Breaking news: A breaking-news report is when you "get the scoop" and report on events that are likely to occur during the upcoming game session. Breaking-news events are things like protester demonstrations, calls for extreme measures in Vietnam, delegate walkouts, or announcements that a delegate intends to enter the race for the presidential or vice presidential nomination. Any breaking-news story must include an on-the-record statement from someone at the center of the story.

Profiles: A profile is an interview with a delegate or protester that includes information about their background and political beliefs. The general public likes these because they humanize their subjects. The best profiles include statements not only from the person being profiled but from others who might know (or have opinions about) that individual.

Investigative journalism: Probably the most challenging type of story to write, an investigative report is when you uncover secrets that delegates or protesters do not want known publicly. All of the delegates and protesters have personal interests that they bring with them to the Convention. Some are even willing to undertake shady actions in order to achieve those interests. Uncovering these secrets is certainly Pulitzer-quality work. But make sure that you have the evidence to substantiate your claims. Libel and slander are serious charges. If charged with either of these offenses, journalists who do not ground their stories in evidence lose the game.

Columns: A column is a piece that expresses one's informed personal opinions. Traditionally, this type of story is reserved for senior-level journalists who have earned the right to state their opinions and not have to obsess with objectivity, but for purposes of the game, *all* journalists write these for their final assignments. They should not be written or submitted to the GM until *after* the final game session. Since these generally enjoy a broad readership, they will have an impact on the general election in November 1968. As with other stories, these should include quotations from individuals and documents that shed light on the topic.

4

PART 4: ROLES AND FACTIONS

DELEGATES

All delegates (except Convention chair Carl Albert) are expected to give speeches from the podium during the Convention. As such, they have podium rights. If they are at the podium, they must be allowed to speak. They are most active during Parts 1, 3, 5, and 7.

Johnson Loyalists

Johnson Loyalists will follow the guidance of the absent president. Although he has stepped back from the presidential race and the Convention, he still possesses significant influence.

Vice President Hubert Humphrey threw his hat into the ring after Johnson announced he would not seek a second term. He is favored to win the presidential nomination and benefits from hundreds of pledge delegates. Consequently, he initially controls more votes than any other role.

Rep. Hale Boggs (La.) is the majority whip in the House of Representatives. In this position, he facilitated the passage of President Johnson's Great Society programs. A staunch anti-communist, he is a strong supporter of the petroleum industry. Despite his initial opposition to the civil rights movement, he decided to support the Voting Rights Act of 1965.

Doves

Doves want an end to the war in Vietnam. They do not necessarily advocate immediate withdrawal, but they certainly support de-escalation.

Sen. Eugene McCarthy (Minn.), known best for his opposition to the Vietnam War, has done well in key primary states, but his successes attracted other antiwar candidates. Many consider him a poor opponent for Nixon. He is a potential presidential nominee.

Sen. Edward "Ted" Kennedy (Mass.) is seen by many as the heir to the Kennedy dynasty. Although he has not officially announced his candidacy, there is a "Draft Ted" movement within the party. His brother Robert was assassinated in June after winning the California primary.

Hawks

Hawks are outspoken supporters of the U.S. war in Vietnam. They do not necessarily want to escalate the war, but they think that the U.S. military must continue to be involved.

Sen. Robert Byrd (W. Va.) is a tireless advocate for his home state, the Constitution, and the virtues of hard work.

Gov. John Connally (Tex.) is a longstanding supporter of President Johnson and (by association) Hubert Humphrey. Accompanying President and Mrs. Kennedy in Dallas, Texas, he was wounded when the president was assassinated in 1963. He is a potential vice president.

Sen. Daniel Inouye (Hawai'i) (pronounced "EE-noh-way") will present the keynote speech for the Convention in Part 3. A decorated WWII veteran, he was the first representative to the U.S. House of Representatives from the new state of Hawai'i.

Civil Rights Activists

Civil Rights Activists are determined to deepen the Democratic Party's commitment to civil rights.

Mrs. Fannie Lou Hamer (Miss.) is a Black civil rights organizer from Mississippi. She gained national attention when she protested the all-white Mississippi delegation at the 1964 Democratic Convention.

Mr. Julian Bond (Ga.) is a Black member of the Georgia House of Representatives. He was a leader in the Student Nonviolent Coordinating Committee (or "SNCC"), a youthful civil rights organization that has taken a radical, Black nationalist turn.

Moderates

Moderates are determined to keep the party united and moving forward.

Mr. Carl Albert (Okla.) is the chairman of the Democratic National Convention, and a strong supporter of Johnson's Great Society programs. He is determined to stage a successful event.

Mayor Richard J. Daley (Ill.) of Chicago is an influential party boss. He has placed the police on high alert to keep order throughout the proceedings of the Convention. His domination of the Illinois delegation and his control over Convention operations give him a great deal of influence.

Sen. Fred Harris (Okla.) is an ambitious populist from a conservative state. He served on the Kerner Commission, which investigated the causes of the violent urban riots that have rocked American cities for the last several years.

Mr. John Bailey (Conn.) is the chairman of the National Democratic Party. He is determined to maintain party unity. His unique ability to convene a Smoke-Filled Room in the middle of Convention proceedings may be key in doing so.

Sen. Edmund "Ed" Muskie (Maine) is an up-and-comer who won office in a traditionally Republican stronghold. He is largely indeterminate.

PROTESTERS

Protesters must remain within the Protest Zone established by Mayor Daley. They are most active during Parts 2, 4, and 6.

Yippies

Yippies are anarchists. They are determined to create a spectacle with their Festival of Life.

Abbie Hoffman is a controversial leader of the Youth International Party or "Yippies." He is no stranger to arrests or police opposition, and is reported to be planning the introduction of the potent hallucinogen LSD into Chicago's water supply.

Jerry Rubin worked with Hoffman to throw dollar bills onto the floor of the New York Stock Exchange. More recently, he worked with David Dellinger to organize an antiwar march on the Pentagon.

Pacifists

Pacifists are dedicated to various forms of nonviolence.

David Dellinger is an experienced activist who is the chair of the National Mobilization Committee against the War (or the "Mobe"). This organization is the antithesis to the unorganized and eccentric protests of the Yippies. It is a coalition of radicals, liberals, and pacifists determined to end the war in Vietnam. He is nonviolent.

Bella Abzug is a leader of the Women's Strike Organization, a group of female protesters opposed to the Vietnam War and pushing for women's rights. She is nonviolent and is known for her magnificent hats.

Allen Ginsberg is a Beat poet. His best-known work is *Howl*, which was banned for indecent language. He has become interested in meditation and Eastern spirituality. He is nonviolent and is skeptical about the efficacy of demonstrations.

Students for a Democratic Society (SDS)

Students for a Democratic Society (SDS) members are dedicated to ending the war and creating a better America for everyone.

Tom Hayden is a founder of SDS and one of the authors of the Port Huron Statement. He is being tailed by plainclothes Chicago police detectives.

Vivian Rothstein is trained in nonviolence. She has worked with civil rights groups like the Student Nonviolent Coordinating Committee (SNCC) and the Congress of Racial Equality (CORE). She is dedicated to social change.

Edward Cox dropped out of Stanford University to join the civil rights movement. Over the years, he has become increasingly radical.

Black Activists

Black Activists want justice for Black Americans. They may have a difficult time swaying other protesters and influencing the Convention because most of the major civil rights organizations opted to stay away from Chicago.

Dick Gregory is a comedian who is committed to civil rights and the antiwar movement. He has announced that he plans to run for president. In advance of the Chicago Convention, he told a group of journalists that unless Chicago passed an open-housing bill and promoted some Black police officers, he intended to lead a nonviolent protest.

Bobby Seale is co-founder of the Black Panther Party, a militant Black Nationalist organization. He demands the end of white violence against Black people.

Indeterminates

Indeterminates are protesters who are still developing their political convictions.

Kathy Boudin (pronounced "BOO-deen") is a college student. She is disenchanted with the establishment and has ceased preparing for medical school. Instead, she has become devoted to social justice.

Fritz Wehrenberg is a student protester camped out at Grant Park; he does not belong to any particular movement. This is his first big political action.

JOURNALISTS

Television Reporters

Television Reporters may submit their stories by posting them in video format. (They should discuss details with the GM before the game begins.)

Dan Rather is an up-and-coming political correspondent for CBS News reporting from the floor of the Convention. He rose to prominence covering the Kennedy assassination in Dallas and travelled to Vietnam in 1966.

Aline Saarinen is one of the first female correspondents for NBC News. Known as an art critic and moderator of *For Women Only,* she has covered a wide range of subjects.

Walter Cronkite, a seasoned reporter, is the anchor of CBS evening news and the "most trusted man in America." He recently broadcast an editorial that characterized Vietnam as a stalemate.

Print Reporters

Print Reporters all work for respected publications. They must distribute their stories in paper form.

Tom Wicker is Washington Bureau Chief of the *New York Times.* His "In the Nation" column is a prominent voice of southern liberalism.

Walter Trohan is a respected and seasoned political reporter for the conservative *Chicago Tribune.* He has served in their Washington bureau for many years, so his depth of knowledge is unrivaled.

Hal Bruno, the news editor for *Newsweek,* has covered stories from around the world, and is pleased to be returning to his hometown, sweet home Chicago.

Mike Royko is a columnist for the Chicago *Daily News.* A lifelong Chicagoan, he is an outspoken critic of the cronyism and corruption of the Daley administration.

Underground Journalists

Underground Journalists usually do not carry much weight inside the Convention Hall or with the American people, but they are very influential in the counterculture. Some of them will publish with mainstream magazines, so their influence is heightened.

Hunter S. Thompson is best known for spending a year riding with a motorcycle gang. He published his findings in *Hell's Angels: The Strange and Terrible Saga of the Outlaw Motorcycle Gangs.* He is collecting information for his next book.

William S. Burroughs is a notorious experimental writer who has been hired by *Esquire Magazine* to cover the Convention.

Paul Krassner writes for *The Realist,* an irreverent, politically radical magazine with a unique measure of raunchy humor and shocking obscenity. He also writes for *Mad,* a satirical monthly that is popular with teenagers.

* * *

The Appendix at the end of the game book (p. 157) describes additional roles, which may be included in your game.

PART 5: CORE TEXTS

CORE TEXTS

Players should familiarize themselves with these texts before the game begins. Once the game has started, they should use them to support the arguments in their speeches and written essays. These are all historical documents, or what historians call "primary sources." The authors often make references without fully explaining them, so I have inserted marginal definitions to clarify their ideas. In a few cases, I have also excerpted from longer documents in order to focus the reading on the central issues of the game.

Players may certainly go beyond these sources, but they must never step into anachronism. Nothing written after September 1968 may be used.

The documents are arranged in chronological order with the most recent text coming first.

CORPORATION COUNSEL OF THE CITY OF CHICAGO

"Biographical Notes Regarding Radical Leaders," September 6, 1968

This report was compiled from Chicago Police Department and Federal Bureau of Investigation records by city officials. It was written after the Convention, but it represents the kind of information that was available to Mayor Daley before the Convention began. It appears here to prepare the authorities for the arrival of the protesters. Mayor Daley may use it to decide whom to apprehend with his plain-clothes detectives.

SOURCE: The Strategy of Confrontation: Chicago and the Democratic National Convention—1968. *United States Department of Justice, 1968, pp. 8–10.*

The following notes give some background on a few of the principals who were involved in confrontation with law enforcement authorities during the week of August 25 to August 30, 1968. These biographical sketches show that they are not strangers to the tactics of confrontation, having been involved in many of the recent mass disorders extending from Berkeley to Columbia to the Pentagon. The outline shows travel to communist countries, draft evasion and disregard for orderly processes of dissent.

Rennie Davis

Rennard (Rennie) Cordon Davis served as local Coordinator of the National Mobilization Committee. He is a chief planner of the Center for Radical Research, a radical left-wing organization; an organizer of Resistance Inside the Army (RITA), which has as its purpose the subversion of military personal within the Army; and actively engaged in the program of Students for Democratic Society (SDS), a radical left-wing organization. Davis, during the month of November, 1967, visited North Vietnam at the invitation of the Hanoi government.

Tom Hayden

Thomas (Tom) E. Hayden is an organizer and former Secretary of the Students for a Democratic Society. He is also an organizer of a group known as the Newark Community Project which was very active during the Newark, New Jersey riots which took place on July 12 through July 17 of 1967. Hayden was referred to by newspapers in New Jersey as the "Maoist Messiah from Michigan". He served behind the scenes at the Columbia University riots and rebellion. Hayden has also visited Hanoi in North Vietnam, against United States policy. His encounters with police in Chicago included resisting arrest and battery on August 27, 1968, obstructing police officers and resisting arrest and disorderly conduct on August 26, 1968. He is considered among the "hip" movement as a violent revolutionary.

Abbie Hoffman

Abbie Hoffman is one of the organizers of the Youth International Party (Yippies). He served as a coordinator of the proposed Festival of Life to be sponsored by the Yippies during the Convention. On May 9, 1968, Hoffman advised a meeting of the Students for Democratic Society of his involvement in the disorders at Columbia University. On May 18, 1967, Hoffman participated in the Washington Square Park (in New York City) march to protest alleged police brutality and to prove that "the streets belong to the people". On November 25, 1967, Hoffman sponsored another demonstration marching from Washington Square Park to Times Square and then to the United Nations in New York, a march alleged to have been conducted by a group known as PTA (Protesters, Terrorists and Anarchists).

Jerry Rubin

Another Yippie leader who devoted his time and talent to bring disruption in the City during the Democratic National Convention was Jerry Rubin. Rubin is a member of the National Coordinating Committee to end the war in Vietnam, which is Communist infiltrated. Rubin visited Cuba during 1964. He attended and was arrested for participating in a demonstration against General Maxwell Taylor on August 24, 1965. He was also arrested for disorderly conduct in Washington, D.C. on August 19, 1966, and in Oakland, California for criminal trespass on November 30, 1966. He was convicted in the student sit-in at the University of California in Berkeley on January 28, 1967. On August 28, 1968, he was arrested at Madison and Dearborn Streets for having led a large group of Yippies who had entered the downtown area and commenced throwing trash cans and garbage into the streets.

David Dellinger

David Dellinger is Chairman of the National Mobilization Committee. He was convicted in 1939 and 1943 for violations of the Selective Service Laws. Dellinger was jailed for ten days by the Washington D.C. police, in a demonstration against the Central Intelligence Agency in 1961. He visited Cuba during the May Day Celebrations in 1964. Dellinger was arrested during a demonstration of the "Assembly of Unrepresented People to Declare Peace in Vietnam" held in Washington D.C. in 1965. He also visited North Vietnam in 1967 contrary to United States policy. He is alleged to have admitted being a Communist.

ABBIE HOFFMAN

"Media Freaking," August 27, 1968

These comments are drawn from a longer interview with Abbie Hoffman, one of the leaders of the Yippies, which was taped by Charles Harbutt at the beginning of the Chicago Democratic Convention and the Festival of Life. This stream-of-consciousness rant begins with his ideas about how to manipulate the police and quickly moves on to describing guerrilla theater and sharing his thoughts about the mass media.

SOURCE: *Charles Harbutt, "Media Freaking,"* The Drama Review: TDR, *vol. 13, no. 4, Politics and Performance, 1969, pp. 46–51.*

This sure is fun. You know, the city news bureau here in Chicago, where you can always call and get their version of what's happening, is ST2-8100. You might want to take care of a cat named Jack Lawrence from CBS who threw me out while I was fuckin' with their teletype machine last night. That was very unfair. I had some good news items.

Now, let's see who else is here. The police, there's some good numbers. OK. Now this is a top secret number that like only a few of the top police have. It's the central number for the police station up here in the zoo. They're very fucked up in there. I've been up there, and you think they're organized, well you're full of shit 'cause their walkie-talkies don't work. I mean they're all stoned up there, tripping over each other, you know, they're **rapping**, all they want to do is fight and they don't care about all the walkie-talkie shit, they just want to fight, you know. That's their thing.

In the late 1960s, **rapping** referred to informal, relaxed conversation.

All right, that number is 528-5967. Now—here's the way you use it. There's a Commander Brash of the 18th Precinct who's in charge of the general area of Lincoln Park and there's Deputy Chief Lynsky who's the cop above him.

Now, the police have a system of anarchy. See, the Chief might say somethin' is OK, see, then you get some low-level **honky** cop saying don't do it, you know. The idea is to convince that honky cop on the other end that Chief Lynsky said it was OK, even if you gotta bullshit him a little. You just drop names, like Commander Brash said this was OK, you know, and if Chief Lynsky said this was OK, you know, those cops don't want to lose their jobs. They won't check it out.

Honky was slang for white person.

Cops are like Yippies—you can never find the leaders. So if you're good at guerrilla theatre, you can look a pig right in the eye and say that to him, you know, and he'll do it. You know, that's the thing, to get him to do it. You just let 'em know that you're stronger psychically than they are. And you *are*, because you came here for nothin' and they're holdin' on to their fuckin' pig jobs 'cause of that little fuckin' paycheck and workin' themselves up, you know. Up to what? To a fuckin' ulcer. Sergeant. We got them by the balls. The whole thing about guerrilla theatre is gettin' them to believe it. Right.

A guy just said that if you make a call, and just leave your phone off the hook, then that line is tied up. That's groovy. I didn't know about that in Chicago. In New York, that doesn't work. I think we ought to be into jamming up all their lines and everythin' and really fuckin' up their communication thing. 'Cause they broke all our walkie-talkies. They made a definite effort to make sure that we can't communicate with each other so like we ought to start communicatin' with them.

Theatre, guerrilla theatre, can be used as defense and as an offensive weapon. I mean, I think like people could survive naked, see. I think you could take all your fuckin' clothes off, a cop won't hit ya. You jump in Lake Michigan, he won't go after you, but people are too chickenshit to do that. It can be used as an offensive and defensive weapon, like blood. We had a demonstration in New York. We had seven gallons of blood in little plastic bags. You know, if you convince 'em you're crazy enough, they won't hurt ya. With the blood thing, cop goes to hit you, right, you have a bag of blood in your hand. He lifts his stick up, you take your bag of blood and go whack over your own head. All this blood pours out, see. Fuckin' cop standin'. Now that says a whole lot more than a picket sign that says end the war in wherever the fuck it is you know.

I mean in that demonstration, there was a fuckin' war there. People came down and looked and said holy shit I don't know what it is, blood all over the fuckin' place, smokebombs goin' off, flares, you know, tape recorders with the sounds of machine guns, cops on horses tramplin' Christmas shoppers. It was a fuckin' *war*. And they say, right, I know what the fuck you're talkin' about. You're talkin' about *war*. What the fuck has a picket line got to do with war?

But people that are into a very literal bag, like that heavy word scene, you know, don't understand the use of communication in this country and the use of media. I mean, if they give a ten-page speech against imperialism, everybody listens and understands and says yeah. But you throw fuckin' money out on the Stock Exchange, and people get that right away. And they say, right, I understand what that's about. And if they don't know what you're doin', fuck 'em. Who cares?

Take this, see, you use blank space as information. You carry a sign that says END THE. You don't need the next word, you just carry a sign that says END, you know. That's enough. I mean the Yippie symbol is Y. So you say, why, man, why, why? Join the Y, bring your sneakers, bring your helmet, right, bring your thing, whatever you got. Y, you say to the Democrats, baby, Y that's not a V it's a Y. You can do a whole lotta shit. Steal it, steal the V, it's a Y. It's up the revolution like that. Keeping your cool and having good wits is your strongest defense.

If you don't want it on TV, write the work "FUCK" on your head, see, and that won't get on TV, right? But that's where theatre is at, it's TV. I mean our thing's for TV. We don't want to get on Meet the Press. What's that shit? We want Ed Sullivan, Johnny Carson show, we want the shit where people are lookin' at it and diggin' it. They're talking about reachin' the troops in Viet Nam so they write in *The Guardian*![1] That's groovy. I've met a *lot* of soldiers who read *The Guardian*, you know. But *we've* had articles in *Jaguar* magazine, *Cavalier*, you know, *National Enquirer* interviews the Queen of the Yippies, someone nobody ever heard of and she runs a whole riff about the Yippies and Viet Nam or whatever her thing is and the soldiers get it and dig it and smoke a little grass and say yeah I can see where she's at.

That's why the long hair. I mean shit, you know, long hair is just another prop. You go on TV and you can say anything you want but the people are lookin' at you and they're lookin' at the cat next to you like David Susskind[2] or some guy like that and they're sayin' hey man there's a choice, I can see it loud and clear. But when they look at a guy from the **Mobilization** and they look at David Susskind, they say well I don't know, they seem to be doing the same thing, can't understand what they're doin'. See, Madison Avenue people think like that. That's why a lot **SDS's** don't like what we're doin'. 'Cause they say we're like exploiting; we're usin' the tools of Madison Ave.[3] But that's because Madison Ave, is effective in what it does. *They* know what the fuck they're doin'. *Meet the Press, Face the Nation, Issues and Answers*—all those bullshit shows, you know, where you get a Democrat and a Republican arguin' right back and forth, this and that, this and that, yeah yeah. But at the end of the show nobody changes their fuckin' mind, you see. But they're tryin' to push Brillo,[4] you see, that's good, you ought to use Brillo, see, and 'bout every ten minutes on will come a three-minute thing of Brillo. Brillo is a revolution, man, Brillo

The National Mobilization Committee to End the War in Vietnam, also known as "the Mobilization," or more succinctly, the **Mobe**, was the main nonviolent antiwar organization.

Students for a Democratic Society, or **SDS**, was a radical antiwar organization.

1. An independent radical newsweekly published in New York.
2. David Susskind hosted *Hot Line*, a New York talk show that often featured controversial guests.
3. Madison Avenue in New York City was the center of the advertising industry.
4. Pop artist Andy Warhol famously made art out of the packaging for Brillo brand scouring pads in 1964. Brillo became a symbol of banal consumerism.

is sex, Brillo is fun, Brillo is bl bl bl bl bl bl bl bl. At the end of the show people ain't fuckin' switchin' from Democrat to Republicans or Commies, you know, the right-wingers or any of that shit. They're buying Brillo! And the reason they have those boring shows is because they don't want to get out any information that'll interfere with Brillo. I mean, can you imagine if they had the Beatles goin' zing zing zing zing zing zing zing, all that jump and shout, you know, and all of a sudden they put on an ad where the guy comes on very straight: "You ought to buy Brillo because it's rationally the correct decision and it's part of the American political process and it's the right way to do things." You know, fuck, they'll buy the Beatles, they won't buy the Brillo.

We taped a thing for the David Susskind Show. As he said the word hippie, a live duck came out with "HIPPIE" painted on it. The duck flew up in the air and shat on the floor and ran all around the room. The only hippie in the room, there he is. And David went crazy. 'Cause David, see, he's *New York Times* head, he's not *Daily News* freak. And he said the duck is out and blew it. We said, we'll see you David, goodnight. He say, oh no no. We'll leave the duck in. And we watched the show later when it came on, and the fuckin' duck was all gone. He done never existed. And I called up Susskind and went quack quack quack, you motherfucker, *that* was the best piece of information: that was a hippie. And everything we did, see, nonverbally, he cut out. Like he said, "How do you eat?" and we fed all the people, you know. But he cut that out. He wants to deal with the words. You know, let's play word games, let's analyze it. Soon as you analyze it, it's dead, it's over. You read a book and say well now I understand it, and go back to sleep.

Hoffman contrasts the staid, mainstream New York Times *with the edgier, picture-heavy tabloid the* Daily News.

The media distorts. But it always works to our advantage. They say there's low numbers, right? 4000, 5000 people here. That's groovy. Think of it, 4000 people causin' all this trouble. If you asked me, I'd say there are four Yippies. I'd say we're bringin' another four on Wednesday. That's good, that freaks 'em out. They're lookin' around. Only four. I mean I saw that trip with the right wing and the Communist conspiracy. You know, you'd have 5000 people out there at the **HUAC** demonstration, eight years ago in San Francisco and they'd say there are five Communists in the crowd, you know. And they did it all. You say, man that's pretty cool. So you just play on their paranoia like that. Yeah, there're four guys out around there doin' a thing. So distortion's gonna backfire on them, 'cause all of a sudden Wednesday by magic there are gonna be 200,000 fuckin' people marchin' on that amphitheatre. That's how many we're gonna have. And they'll say, "Wow. From 4000 up to 200,000. Those extra four Yippies did a hell of a good job."

The House Un-American Activities Committee, or **HUAC**, held hearings in San Francisco in May 1960 that were intended to investigate "communist subversion." The result was protests.

I dig that, see. I'm not interested in explainin' my way of life to straight people or people that aren't interested. They never gonna understand it anyway and I couldn't explain it anyway.

All I know is, in terms of images and how words are used as images to shape your environment, the *New York Times* is death to us. That's the worst fuckin' paper as far as the Yippies are concerned. They say, "Members of the so-called Youth

International Party held a demonstration today." That ain't nothin'. What fuckin' people read that? They fall asleep. 'Cause the *New York Times* has all the news that's fit to print, you know, so once they have all the news, what do the people have to do? They just read the *New York Times* and drink their coffee and go back to work, you know. But the *Daily News*, that's a TV set. Look at it, I mean look at the picture right up front and the way they blast those headlines. You know, "Yippies, sex-loving, dope-loving, commie, beatnik, hippie, freako, weirdos." That's groovy, man, that's a whole life style, that's a whole thing to be, man. I mean you want to get in on that.

When we stormed the Pentagon, my wife and I we leaped over this fence, see. We were really stoned, I mean I was on acid flying away, which of course is an anti-revolutionary drug you know, you can't do a thing on it.[5] I've been on acid ever since I came to Chicago. It's in the form of honey. We got a lab guy doin' his thing. I think he might have got assassinated, I ain't seen him today. Well, so we jumped this here fence, see, we were sneaking through the woods and people were out to get the Pentagon. We had this flag, it said NOW with a big wing on it, I don't know. The right-wingers said there was definitely evidence of Communist conspiracy 'cause of that flag, I don't know what the fuck it was. So we had Uncle Sam hats on, you know, and we jumped over the fence and we're surrounded by marshals, you know, just closin' us in, about 30 marshals around us. And I plant the fuckin' flag and I said, "I claim this land in the name of free America. We are Mr. and Mrs. America. Mrs. America's pregnant." And we sit down and they're goin' fucking crazy. I mean we got arrested and unarrested like six or seven times. And when we finally got arrested, it was under other names. I'm really a digger,[6] I never was a Yippie. Was always a digger. So I said, you know, A. Digger, Abbie Digger, Mr. and Mrs. A. Digger. They say are you a boy or a girl, I say girl. Right. This is where I wanna go. I don't have to prove manliness by beatin' up 14-year-old girls with nightsticks, you know. Fuck 'em. But ideas, you just get stoned, get the ideas in your head and then do 'em. And don't bullshit. I mean that's the thing about doin' that guerrilla theatre. You be prepared to die to prove your point. You gotta die.

In October 1967, Hoffman participated in a massive antiwar march on the Pentagon in Washington, D.C.

You know, what's life? Life's all that fun shit. Life's doin' what you want to do. *Life*'s an American magazine, and if we hook them right, they're gonna give us 10,000 flowers that are gonna be thrown out of a helicopter tomorrow afternoon. But we'll only allow them to do it if they bring a newsreel person up in the helicopter with 'em. You know, to take the pictures. So we're workin' out that negotiation with *Life* magazine. 'Cause we said, you know, it's called Festival of Life, man, we named it after your magazine. I know that's immoral and I know that's cheatin' and that's stealin'. I wish I was a revolutionist. I wouldn't have these problems. A lot of revolutionists come here, they worry about parking the car. Where we gonna park the car, should we park it in a meter? The meter'll run out, we'll get a ticket. It's a weird revolution.

5. Lysergic acid diethylamide (LSD), or "acid," is a potent and illegal hallucinogen.

6. The Diggers were a radical street theater group in San Francisco.

Fuck it. We don't need cars; we travel in wheelbarrows. You see, just worry about your ass. Forget about your clothes, your money, you know, just worry about your ass and all the rest of us's asses. Cars don't mean shit. They grab our walkie-talkies you say yeah, there you go, take it, thank you, it was too heavy to carry.

I think it's a good idea to cut your hair or get a wig or let your hair grow pretty fast or paint your face or change your clothes or get a new hat and a new name. I mean everybody ought to have a new name by Wednesday. And like you know we're all one huge happy family with all new names or no names and no faces. 'Cause when we bust out of this park and go down to Grant Park and then go out to the amphitheatre, there are gonna be some mighty strange theatrical events. And you better have your theatre thing down pretty pat.

Well, I've shot my load. I'm for ending the Yippie thing Thursday, killin' it all, 'cause I don't think people are Yippies anymore than they're Mobe or Mother-fuckers or whatever they are. They're just people. And I think we oughta burn all our Yippie buttons and laugh at the fuckin' press and say nyah nyah, we took you for a fuckin' ride. That's what we figured when we started this thing back in December—just a couple of speedfreaks hangin' around the cellar sayin' now how are we gonna do this Chicago trip? We ain't got no fuckin' money, you know, we ain't got no organization, we ain't got no constituency. We went to a New Left meeting, they said where's your constituency, you can't talk here, you know, you ain't against imperialism. I said, man, I don't want any pay toilets in this fuckin' country, I don't want to pay a dime to take a shit. SDS doesn't consider that relevant. That's the trouble with the Left you know. Did a trip on a Socialist Scholars Conference, a couple of **Hell's Angels** guys and I, we went up and had a capgun fight in the Hotel Hilton where the Left has their conferences, it's very interesting. So the heads of the Hilton and the heads of the socialists were gettin' together to decide how to throw us speedfreaks out of the fuckin' place, see. But they didn't, I mean, we stayed to do our thing.

Hell's Angels is a notorious motorcycle gang.

The problem with the Left is that there are 10,000 socialist scholars in this country and not one fuckin' socialist. I mean I talk to guys on *The Guardian* and they say yeah, we're working on a serious analysis of the Yippies. I say, that's pretty fuckin' cool, man, that's great. By that time there won't be any Yippies. I mean, what the fuck are you analyzin' for, man, get in and do it.

RICHARD NIXON

"Address Accepting the Presidential Nomination," August 8, 1968

In the Republican Convention, which concluded a few weeks before the Democratic Convention began, Nixon was challenged by Governor Ronald Reagan of California and Governor Nelson Rockefeller of New York. An early challenger, Governor George Romney of Michigan, dropped out of the race because he committed the campaign gaffe of stating that he had been "brainwashed" by military officials during a 1965 visit to South Vietnam.

Nixon prevailed at the convention due to his appeal to the "silent majority" for law and order, his vague promises to extricate the United States from the war in Vietnam, and his commitment to "peaceful competition" with the Soviet Union and the People's Republic of China. These carried the day with the party faithful, but in polls taken after the convention only 43 percent of Americans supported his candidacy.

SOURCE: *Richard Nixon, "Address Accepting the Presidential Nomination at the Republican National Convention in Miami Beach, Florida." Posted online by Gerhard Peters and John T. Woolley, The American Presidency Project.*

Mr. Chairman, delegates to this convention, my fellow Americans.

Sixteen years ago I stood before this Convention to accept your nomination as the running mate of one of the greatest Americans of our time—or of any time—Dwight D. Eisenhower.

Eight years ago, I had the highest honor of accepting your nomination for President of the United States.

Tonight, I again proudly accept that nomination for President of the United States.

But I have news for you. This time there is a difference.

This time we are going to win.

We're going to win for a number of reasons: first a personal one. General Eisenhower, as you know, lies critically ill in the Walter Reed Hospital tonight. I have talked, however, with Mrs. Eisenhower on the telephone. She tells me that his heart is with us. And she says that there is nothing that he lives more for and there is nothing that would lift him more than for us to win in November and I say let's win this one for Ike!

We are going to win because this great Convention has demonstrated to the nation that the Republican Party has the leadership, the platform and the purpose that America needs.

We are going to win because you have nominated as my running mate a statesman of the first rank who will be a great campaigner and one who is fully qualified to undertake the new responsibilities that I shall give to the next Vice President of the United States.[1]

And he is a man who fully shares my conviction and yours, that after a period of forty years when power has gone from the cities and the states to the government in Washington, D.C., it's time to have power go back from Washington to the states and to the cities of this country all over America.

---

1. Spiro Agnew, the governor of Maryland, was Nixon's running mate.

We are going to win because at a time that America cries out for the unity that this Administration has destroyed, the Republican Party—after a spirited contest for its nomination for President and for Vice President—stands united before the nation tonight.

I congratulate Governor Reagan. I congratulate Governor Rockefeller. I congratulate Governor Romney. I congratulate all those who have made the hard fight that they have for this nomination. And I know that you will all fight even harder for the great victory our party is going to win in November because we're going to be together in that election campaign.

And a party that can unite itself will unite America.

My fellow Americans, most important—we are going to win because our cause is right.

We make history tonight—not for ourselves but for the ages.

The choice we make in 1968 will determine not only the future of America but the future of peace and freedom in the world for the last third of the twentieth century.

And the question that we answer tonight: can America meet this great challenge?

For a few moments, let us look at America, let us listen to America to find the answer to that question.

As we look at America, we see cities enveloped in smoke and flame.

We hear sirens in the night.

We see Americans dying on distant battlefields abroad.

We see Americans hating each other; fighting each other; killing each other at home.

And as we see and hear these things, millions of Americans cry out in anguish.

Did we come all this way for this?

Did American boys die in Normandy, and Korea, and in Valley Forge for this?[2]

Listen to the answer to those questions.

It is another voice. It is the quiet voice in the tumult and the shouting.

It is the voice of the great majority of Americans, the forgotten Americans—the non-shouters; the non-demonstrators.

They are not racists or sick; they are not guilty of the crime that plagues the land.

They are black and they are white—they're native born and foreign born—they're young and they're old.

They work in America's factories.

They run America's businesses.

They serve in government.

They provide most of the soldiers who died to keep us free.

---

2. These were all moments of particularly determined effort on the part of the U.S. military.

They give drive to the spirit of America.

They give lift to the American Dream.

They give steel to the backbone of America.

They are good people, they are decent people; they work, and they save, and they pay their taxes, and they care.

Like Theodore Roosevelt, they know that this country will not be a good place for any of us to live in unless it is a good place for all of us to live in.

This I say to you tonight is the real voice of America. In this year 1968, this is the message it will broadcast to America and to the world.

Let's never forget that despite her faults, America is a great nation.

And America is great because her people are great.

With Winston Churchill, we say: "We have not journeyed all this way across the centuries, across the oceans, across the mountains, across the prairies because we are made of sugar candy."

America is in trouble today not because her people have failed but because her leaders have failed.

And what America needs are leaders to match the greatness of her people.

And this great group of Americans, the forgotten Americans, and others know that the great question Americans must answer by their votes in November is this: Whether we shall continue for four more years the policies of the last five years.

And this is their answer and this is my answer to that question.

When the strongest nation in the world can be tied down for four years in a war in Vietnam with no end in sight;

When the richest nation in the world can't manage its own economy;

When the nation with the greatest tradition of the rule of law is plagued by unprecedented lawlessness;

When a nation that has been known for a century for equality of opportunity is tom by unprecedented racial violence;

And when the President of the United States cannot travel abroad or to any major city at home without fear of a hostile demonstration—then it's time for new leadership for the United States of America.

My fellow Americans, tonight I accept the challenge and the commitment to provide that new leadership for America.

And I ask you to accept it with me.

And let us accept this challenge not as a grim duty but as an exciting adventure in which we are privileged to help a great nation realize its destiny.

And let us begin by committing ourselves to the truth—to see it like it is, and tell it like it is—to find the truth, to speak the truth, and to live the truth—that's what we will do.

We've had enough of big promises and little action.

The time has come for honest government in the United States of America.

And so tonight I do not promise the millennium in the morning.

I don't promise that we can eradicate poverty, and end discrimination, eliminate all danger of war in the space of four, or even eight years. But, I do promise action—a new policy for peace abroad; a new policy for peace and progress and justice at home.

Look at our problems abroad. Do you realize that we face the stark truth that we are worse off in every area of the world tonight than we were when President Eisenhower left office eight years ago. That's the record. And there is only one answer to such a record of failure and that is a complete housecleaning of those responsible for the failures of that record. The answer is a complete re-appraisal of America's policies in every section of the world.

We shall begin with Vietnam.

We all hope in this room that there is a chance that current negotiations may bring an honorable end to that war. And we will say nothing during this campaign that might destroy that chance.

But if the war is not ended when the people choose in November, the choice will be clear. Here it is.

For four years this Administration has had at its disposal the greatest military and economic advantage that one nation has ever had over another in any war in history.

For four years, America's fighting men have set a record for courage and sacrifice unsurpassed in our history.

For four years, this Administration has had the support of the Loyal Opposition for the objective of seeking an honorable end to the struggle.

Never has so much military and economic and diplomatic power been used so ineffectively.

And if after all of this time and all of this sacrifice and all of this support there is still no end in sight, then I say the time has come for the American people to turn to new leadership—not tied to the mistakes and the policies of the past. That is what we offer to America.

And I pledge to you tonight that the first priority foreign policy objective of our next Administration will be to bring an honorable end to the war in Vietnam. We shall not stop there—we need a policy to prevent more Vietnams.

All of America's peace-keeping institutions and all of America's foreign commitments must be re-appraised. Over the past twenty-five years, America has provided more than one hundred and fifty billion dollars in foreign aid to nations abroad.

In Korea and now again in Vietnam, the United States furnished most of the money, most of the arms; most of the men to help the people of those countries defend themselves against aggression.

Now we are a rich country. We are a strong nation. We are a populous nation. But there are two hundred million Americans and there are two billion people that live in the Free World.

And I say the time has come for other nations in the Free World to bear their fair share of the burden of defending peace and freedom around this world.

What I call for is not a new isolationism. It is a new internationalism in which America enlists its allies and its friends around the world in those struggles in which their interest is as great as ours.

And now to the leaders of the Communist world, we say: After an era of confrontation, the time has come for an era of negotiation.

Where the world's super powers are concerned, there is no acceptable alternative to peaceful negotiation.

Because this will be a period of negotiation, we shall restore the strength of America so that we shall always negotiate from strength and never from weakness.

And as we seek peace through negotiation, let our goals be made clear:

We do not seek domination over any other country.

We believe deeply in our ideas, but we believe they should travel on their own power and not on the power of our arms.

We shall never be belligerent but we shall be as firm in defending our system as they are in expanding theirs.

We believe this should be an era of peaceful competition, not only in the productivity of our factories but in the quality of our ideas.

We extend the hand of friendship to all people, to the Russian people, to the Chinese people, to all people in the world.

And we shall work toward the goal of an open world—open skies, open cities, open hearts, open minds.

The next eight years, my friends, this period in which we are entering, I think we will have the greatest opportunity for world peace but also face the greatest danger of world war of any time in our history.

I believe we must have peace. I believe that we can have peace, but I do not underestimate the difficulty of this task. Because you see the art of preserving peace is greater than that of waging war and much more demanding. But I am proud to have served in an Administration which ended one war and kept the nation out of other wars for eight years. And it is that kind of experience and it is that kind of leadership that America needs today, and that we will give to America with your help.

And as we commit to new policies for America tonight, let us make one further pledge:

For five years hardly a day has gone by when we haven't read or heard a report of the American flag being spit on; an embassy being stoned; a library being burned; or an ambassador being insulted some place in the world. And each incident reduced respect for the United States until the ultimate insult inevitably occurred.

And I say to you tonight that when respect for the United States of America falls so low that a fourth-rate military power, like North Korea, will seize an

American naval vessel on the high seas, it is time for new leadership to restore respect for the United States of America.[3]

My friends, America is a great nation.

And it is time we started to act like a great nation around the world. It is ironic to note when we were a small nation—weak military and poor economically—America was respected. And the reason was that America stood for something more powerful than military strength or economic wealth.

The American Revolution was a shining example of freedom in action which caught the imagination of the world.

Today, too often, America is an example to be avoided and not followed.

A nation that can't keep the peace at home won't be trusted to keep the peace abroad.

A President who isn't treated with respect at home will not be treated with respect abroad.

A nation which can't manage its own economy can't tell others how to manage theirs.

If we are to restore prestige and respect for America abroad, the place to begin is at home in the United States of America.

My friends, we live in an age of revolution in America and in the world. And to find the answers to our problems, let us turn to a revolution, a revolution that will never grow old. The world's greatest continuing revolution, the American Revolution.

The American Revolution was and is dedicated to progress, but our founders recognized that the first requisite of progress is order.

Now, there is no quarrel between progress and order—because neither can exist without the other.

So let us have order in America—not the order that suppresses dissent and discourages change but the order which guarantees the right to dissent and provides the basis for peaceful change.

And tonight, it is time for some honest talk about the problem of order in the United States.

Let us always respect, as I do, our courts and those who serve on them. But let us also recognize that some of our courts in their decisions have gone too far in weakening the peace forces as against the criminal forces in this country and we must act to restore that balance.

Let those who have the responsibility to enforce our laws and our judges who have the responsibility to interpret them be dedicated to the great principles of civil rights.

---

3. Nixon is referring to the January 1968 seizure of the *USS Pueblo*—a spy ship. The crew was still held in North Korea in August 1968.

But let them also recognize that the first civil right of every American is to be free from domestic violence, and that right must be guaranteed in this country.

And if we are to restore order and respect for law in this country there is one place we are going to begin. We are going to have a new Attorney General of the United States of America.

I pledge to you that our new Attorney General will be directed by the President of the United States to launch a war against organized crime in this country.

I pledge to you that our new Attorney General of the United States will be an active belligerent against the loan sharks and the numbers racketeers that rob the urban poor in our cities.

I pledge to you that the new Attorney General will open a new front against the filth peddlers and the narcotics peddlers who are corrupting the lives of the children of this country.

Because, my friends, let this message come through clear from what I say tonight. Time is running out for the merchants of crime and corruption in American society.

The wave of crime is not going to be the wave of the future in the United States of America.

We shall re-establish freedom from fear in America so that America can take the lead in re-establishing freedom from fear in the world.

And to those who say that law and order is the code word for racism, there and here is a reply:

Our goal is justice for every American.

If we are to have respect for law in America, we must have laws that deserve respect.

Just as we cannot have progress without order, we cannot have order without progress, and so, as we commit to order tonight, let us commit to progress.

And this brings me to the clearest choice among the great issues of this campaign.

For the past five years we have been deluged by government programs for the unemployed; programs for the cities; programs for the poor. And we have reaped from these programs an ugly harvest of frustration, violence and failure across the land.

Here Nixon criticizes Johnson's Great Society programs.

And now our opponents will be offering more of the same—more billions for government jobs, government housing, government welfare.

I say it is time to quit pouring billions of dollars into programs that have failed in the United States of America.

To put it bluntly, we are on the wrong road—and it's time to take a new road, to progress.

Again, we turn to the American Revolution for our answer.

The war on poverty didn't begin five years ago in this country. It began when this country began. It's been the most successful war on poverty in the history of nations. There is more wealth in America today, more broadly shared, than in any nation in the world.

We are a great nation. And we must never forget how we became great.

America is a great nation today not because of what government did for people—but because of what people did for themselves over a hundred ninety years in this country.

So it is time to apply the lessons of the American Revolution to our present problem.

Let us increase the wealth of America so that we can provide more generously for the aged; and for the needy; and for all those who cannot help themselves.

But for those who are able to help themselves—what we need are not more millions on welfare rolls—but more millions on payrolls in the United States of America.

Instead of government jobs, and government housing, and government welfare, let government use its tax and credit policies to enlist in this battle the greatest engine of progress ever developed in the history of man—American private enterprise.

Let us enlist in this great cause the millions of Americans in volunteer organizations who will bring a dedication to this task that no amount of money could ever buy.

And let us build bridges, my friends, build bridges to human dignity across that gulf that separates black America from white America.

Black Americans, no more than white Americans, they do not want more government programs which perpetuate dependency.

They don't want to be a colony in a nation.

They want the pride, and the self-respect, and the dignity that can only come if they have an equal chance to own their own homes, to own their own businesses, to be managers and executives as well as workers, to have a piece of the action in the exciting ventures of private enterprise.

I pledge to you tonight that we shall have new programs which will provide that equal chance.

We make great history tonight.

We do not fire a shot heard 'round the world but we shall light the lamp of hope in millions of homes across this land in which there is no hope today.

And that great light shining out from America will again become a beacon of hope for all those in the world who seek freedom and opportunity.

My fellow Americans, I believe that historians will recall that 1968 marked the beginning of the American generation in world history.

Just to be alive in America, just to be alive at this time is an experience unparalleled in history. Here is where the action is. Think.

Thirty-two years from now most Americans living today will celebrate a new year that comes once in a thousand years.

Eight years from now, in the second term of the next President, we will celebrate the 200th anniversary of the American Revolution.

And by our decision in this election, we, all of us here, all of you listening on television and radio, we will determine what kind of nation America will be on its 200th birthday; we will determine what kind of a world America will live in in the year 2000.

This is the kind of a day I see for America on that glorious Fourth—eight years from now.

I see a day when Americans are once again proud of their flag. When once again at home and abroad, it is honored as the world's greatest symbol of liberty and justice.

I see a day when the President of the United States is respected and his office is honored because it is worthy of respect and worthy of honor.

I see a day when every child in this land, regardless of his background, has a chance for the best education our wisdom and schools can provide, and an equal chance to go just as high as his talents will take him.

I see a day when life in rural America attracts people to the country, rather than driving them away.

I see a day when we can look back on massive breakthroughs in solving the problems of slums and pollution and traffic which are choking our cities to death.

I see a day when our senior citizens and millions of others can plan for the future with the assurance that their government is not going to rob them of their savings by destroying the value of their dollars.

I see a day when we will again have freedom from fear in America and freedom from fear in the world.

I see a day when our nation is at peace and the world is at peace and everyone on earth—those who hope, those who aspire, those who crave liberty—will look to America as the shining example of hopes realized and dreams achieved.

My fellow Americans, this is the cause I ask you to vote for. This is the cause I ask you to work for. This is the cause I ask you to commit to—not just for victory in November but beyond that to a new Administration.

Because the time when one man or a few leaders could save America is gone. We need tonight nothing less than the total commitment and the total mobilization of the American people if we are to succeed.

Government can pass laws. But respect for law can come only from people who take the law into their hearts and their minds—and not into their hands.

Government can provide opportunity. But opportunity means nothing unless people are prepared to seize it.

A president can ask for reconciliation in the racial conflict that divides Americans. But reconciliation comes only from the hearts of people.

And tonight, therefore, as we make this commitment, let us look into our hearts and let us look down into the faces of our children.

Is there anything in the world that should stand in their way?

None of the old hatreds mean anything when we look down into the faces of our children.

In their faces is our hope, our love, and our courage.

Tonight, I see the face of a child.

He lives in a great city. He is black. Or he is white. He is Mexican, Italian, Polish. None of that matters. What matters, he's an American child.

That child in that great city is more important than any politician's promise. He is America. He is a poet. He is a scientist, he is a great teacher, he is a proud craftsman. He is everything we ever hoped to be and everything we dare to dream to be.

He sleeps the sleep of childhood and he dreams the dreams of a child.

And yet when he awakens, he awakens to a living nightmare of poverty, neglect and despair.

He fails in school.

He ends up on welfare.

For him the American system is one that feeds his stomach and starves his soul. It breaks his heart. And in the end it may take his life on some distant battlefield.

To millions of children in this rich land, this is their prospect of the future.

But this is only part of what I see in America.

I see another child tonight.

He hears the train go by at night and he dreams of faraway places where he'd like to go.

It seems like an impossible dream.

But he is helped on his journey through life.

A father who had to go to work before he finished the sixth grade, sacrificed everything he had so that his sons could go to college.

A gentle, Quaker mother, with a passionate concern for peace, quietly wept when he went to war but she understood why he had to go.

A great teacher, a remarkable football coach, an inspirational minister encouraged him on his way.

A courageous wife and loyal children stood by him in victory and also defeat.

And in his chosen profession of politics, first there were scores, then hundreds, then thousands, and finally millions worked for his success.

And tonight he stands before you—nominated for President of the United States of America.

You can see why I believe so deeply in the American Dream.

For most of us the American Revolution has been won; the American Dream has come true.

And what I ask you to do tonight is to help me make that dream come true for millions to whom it's an impossible dream today.

One hundred and eight years ago, the newly elected President of the United States, Abraham Lincoln, left Springfield, Illinois, never to return again. He spoke to his friends gathered at the railroad station. Listen to his words:

"Today I leave you. I go to assume a greater task than devolved on General Washington. The great God which helped him must help me. Without that great assistance, I will surely fail. With it, I cannot fail."

Abraham Lincoln lost his life but he did not fail.

The next President of the United States will face challenges which in some ways will be greater than those of Washington or Lincoln. Because for the first time in our nation's history, an American President will face not only the problem of restoring peace abroad but of restoring peace at home.

Without God's help and your help, we will surely fail; but with God's help and your help, we shall surely succeed.

My fellow Americans, the long dark night for America is about to end.

The time has come for us to leave the valley of despair and climb the mountain so that we may see the glory of the dawn—a new day for America, and a new dawn for peace and freedom in the world.

NATIONAL ADVISORY COMMISSION ON CIVIL DISORDERS

Kerner Report Excerpts, February 29, 1968

In July 1967, President Lyndon B. Johnson appointed an eleven-member National Advisory Commission on Civil Disorders to explain the riots that plagued U.S. cities since 1964 and to provide recommendations for the future. He asked for answers to three basic questions about the riots: What happened? Why did it happen? What can be done to prevent it from happening again and again? The lengthy report quickly became a best-seller.

Quite harsh in its criticisms of federal policy, white racism, and media coverage of the riots, the report offered a number of specific recommendations. Martin Luther King Jr. called it a "physician's warning of approaching death, with a prescription for life." However, Johnson did not implement any of the recommendations. One month after the report was issued, the assassination of Martin Luther King Jr. led to riots in over 100 American cities.

Senator Fred Harris, who may be in the game, was a member of the Commission.

SOURCE: *The National Advisory Commission on Civil Disorders,* The Kerner Report, *Princeton University Press, 2016, pp. 1–11, 18–28, 30, 364–368. Originally published by the U.S. Government Printing Office, 1968.*

INTRODUCTION

The summer of 1967 again brought racial disorders to American cities, and with them shock, fear, and bewilderment to the Nation.

The worst came during a 2-week period in July, first in Newark and then in Detroit. Each set off a chain reaction in neighboring communities.

On July 28, 1967, the President of the United States established this Commission and directed us to answer three basic questions:

What happened?
Why did it happen?
What can be done to prevent it from happening again?

To respond to these questions, we have undertaken a broad range of studies and investigations. We have visited the riot cities; we have heard many witnesses; we have sought the counsel of experts across the country.

This is our basic conclusion: Our Nation is moving toward two societies, one black, one white—separate and unequal.

Reaction to last summer's disorders has quickened the movement and deepened the division. Discrimination and segregation have long permeated much of American life; they now threaten the future of every American.

This deepening racial division is not inevitable. The movement apart can be reversed. Choice is still possible. Our principal task is to define that choice and to press for a national resolution.

To pursue our present course will involve the continuing polarization of the American community and, ultimately, the destruction of basic democratic values.

The alternative is not blind repression or capitulation to lawlessness. It is the realization of common opportunities for all within a single society.

This alternative will require a commitment to national action—compassionate, massive, and sustained, backed by the resources of the most powerful and the richest nation on this earth. From every American it will require new attitudes, new understanding, and, above all, new will.

The vital needs of the Nation must be met; hard choices must be made, and, if necessary, new taxes enacted.

Violence cannot build a better society. Disruption and disorder nourish repression, not justice. They strike at the freedom of every citizen. The community cannot—it will not—tolerate coercion and mob rule.

Violence and destruction must be ended—in the streets of the ghetto and in the lives of people.

Segregation and poverty have created in the racial ghetto a destructive environment totally unknown to most white Americans.

What white Americans have never fully understood—but what the Negro can never forget—is that white society is deeply implicated in the ghetto. White institutions created it, white institutions maintain it, and white society condones it.

It is time now to turn with all the purpose at our command to the major unfinished business of this Nation. It is time to adopt strategies for action that will produce quick and visible progress. It is time to make good the promises of American democracy to all citizens: urban and rural, white and black, Spanish-surname, American Indian, and every minority group.

Our recommendations embrace three basic principles:

- To mount programs on a scale equal to the dimension of the problems;
- To aim these programs for high impact in the immediate future in order to close the gap between promise and performance;
- To undertake new initiatives and experiment that can change the system of failure and frustration that now dominates the ghetto and weakens our society.

These programs will require unprecedented levels of funding and performance, but they neither probe deeper nor demand more than the problems which called them forth. There can be no higher priority for national action and no higher claim on the Nation's conscience.

* * *

I. WHAT HAPPENED?

Chapter 1.—Profiles of Disorder

The report contains profiles of a selection of the disorders that took place during the summer of 1967. These profiles are designed to indicate how the disorders happened, who participated in them, and how local officials, police forces, and the National Guard responded. Illustrative excerpts follow:

* * *

[. . .] On Saturday, July 15, [Director of Police Dominick] Spina received a report of snipers in a housing project. When he arrived he saw approximately 100 National

The first selection describes the ways in which nervous National Guardsmen escalated the situation after being deployed in Newark, New Jersey, in July 1967.

Guardsmen and police officers crouching behind vehicles, hiding in corners, and lying on the ground around the edge of the courtyard.

Since everything appeared quiet and it was broad daylight. Spina walked directly down the middle of the street. Nothing happened. As he came to the last building of the complex, he heard a shot. All around him the troopers jumped, believing themselves to be under sniper fire. A moment later a young Guardsman ran from behind a building.

The director of police went over and asked him if he had fired the shot. The soldier said "Yes," he had fired to scare a man away from a window; that his orders were to keep everyone away from windows.

Spina said he told the soldier: "Do you know what you just did? You have now created a state of hysteria. Every Guardsman up and down this street and every state policeman and every city policeman that is present thinks that somebody just fired a shot and that it is probably a sniper."

A short time later more "gunshots" were heard. Investigating. Spina came upon a Puerto Rican sitting on a wall. In reply to a question as to whether he knew "where the firing is coming from?" the man said:

"That's no firing. That's fireworks. If you look up to the fourth floor, you will see the people who are throwing down these cherry bombs."

By this time four trucklonds of National Guardsmen had arrived and troopers and policemen were again crouched everywhere looking for a sniper. The director of police remained at the scene for 3 hours, and the only shot fired was the one by the Guardsman.

Nevertheless, at 6 o'clock that evening two columns of National Guardsmen and State troopers were directing mass fire at the Hayes housing project in response to what they believed were snipers. [. . .]

Detroit

[. . .] A spirit of carefree nihilism was taking hold. To riot and destroy appeared more and more to become ends in themselves. Late Sunday afternoon it appeared to one observer that the young people were "dancing amidst the flames."

A Negro plainclothes officer was standing at an intersection when a man threw a Molotov cocktail into a business establishment at the corner. In the heat of the afternoon, fanned by the 20 to 25 miles per hour winds of both Sunday and Monday, the fire reached the home next door within minutes. As residents uselessly sprayed the flames with garden hoses, the fire jumped from roof to roof of adjacent two- and three-story buildings. Within the hour the entire block was in flames. The ninth house in the burning row belonged to the arsonist who had thrown the Molotov cocktail. [. . .]

The description of the Detroit riot describes a wide variety of responses by the residents.

* * *

[. . .] Employed as a private guard, 55-year-old Julius L. Dorsey, a Negro, was standing in front of a market when accosted by two Negro men and a woman. They demanded he permit them to loot the market. He ignored their demands. They began to berate him. He asked a neighbor to call the police. As the argument grew more heated, Dorsey fired three shots from his pistol into the air.

The Report *stresses the determination with which some residents attempted to stop the riot.*

The police radio reported: "Looters—they have rifles." A patrol car driven by a police officer and carrying three National Guardsmen arrived. As the looters fled, the law-enforcement personnel opened fire. When the firing ceased, one person lay dead.

He was Julius L. Dorsey [. . .]

* * *

[. . .] As the riot alternately waxed and waned, one area of the ghetto remained insulated. On the northeast side the residents of some 150 square blocks inhabited by 21,000 persons had, in 1966, banded together in the Positive Neighborhood Action Committee (PNAC). With professional help from the Institute of Urban Dynamics, they had organized block clubs and made plans for the improvement of the neighborhood. [. . .]

When the riot broke out, the residents, through the block clubs, were able to organize quickly. Youngsters, agreeing to stay in the neighborhood, participated in detouring traffic. While many persons reportedly sympathized with the idea of a rebellion against the "system" only two small fires were set—one in an empty building.

* * *

[. . .] According to Lieutenant General Throckmorton and Colonel Bolling, the city, at this time, was saturated with fear. The National Guardsmen were afraid, the citizens were afraid, and the police were afraid. Numerous persons, the majority of them Negroes, were being injured by gunshots of undermined origin. The general and his staff felt that the major task of the troops was to reduce the fear and restore an air of normaley.

The Report *also describes episodes of cooperation between residents and National Guardsmen.*

In order to accomplish this, every effort was made to establish contact and rapport between the troops and the residents. The soldiers—20 percent of whom were Negro—began helping to clean up the streets, collect garbage, and trace persons who had disappeared in the confusion. Residents in the neighborhoods responded with soup and sandwiches for the troops. In areas where the National Guard tried to establish rapport with the citizens, there was a similar response.

* * *

In addition to documenting the specifics of the situations in Newark and Detroit, the Report *sought to describe common features of Black unrest throughout the nation.*

Chapter 2.—Patterns of Disorder

The "typical" riot did not take, place. The disorders of 1967 were unusual, irregular, complex, and unpredictable social processes. Like most human events, they did not unfold in an orderly sequence. However, an analysis of our survey information leads to some conclusions about the riot process.

In general:

- The civil disorders of 1967 involved Negroes acting against local symbols of white American society, authority, and property in Negro neighborhoods—rather than against white persons.
- Of 164 disorders reported during the first nine months of 1967, eight (5 percent) were major in terms of violence and damage; 33 (20 percent) were serious but not major; 123 (75 percent) were minor and undoubtedly would not have received national attention as riots had the Nation not been sensitized by the more serious outbreaks.
- In the 75 disorders studied by a Senate subcommittee, 83 deaths were reported. Eighty-two percent of the deaths and more than half the injuries occurred in Newark and Detroit. About 10 percent of the dead and 36 percent of the injured were public employees, primarily law officers and firemen. The overwhelming majority of the persons killed or injured in all the disorders were Negro civilians.
- Initial damage estimates were greatly exaggerated. In Detroit, newspaper damage estimates at first ranged from $200 to $500 million; the highest recent estimate is $45 million. In Newark, early estimates ranged from $15 to $25 million. A month later damage was estimated at $10.2 million, 80 percent in inventory losses.

In the 24 disorders in 23 cities which we surveyed:

- The final incident before the outbreak of disorder, and the initial violence itself, generally took place in the evening or at night at a place in which it was normal for many people to be on the streets.
- Violence usually occurred almost immediately following the occurrence of the final precipitating incident, and then escalated rapidly. With but few exceptions, violence subsided during the day, and flared rapidly again at night. The night-day cycles continued through the early period of the major disorders.
- Disorder generally began with rock and bottle throwing and window breaking. Once store windows were broken, looting usually followed.
- Disorder did not erupt as a result of a single "triggering" or "precipitating" incident. Instead, it was generated out of an increasingly disturbed

social atmosphere, in which typically a series of tension-heightening incidents over a period of weeks or months became linked in the minds of many in the Negro community with a reservoir of underlying grievances. At some point in the mounting tension, a further incident—in itself often routine or trivial—became the breaking point and the tension spilled over into violence.

- "Prior" incidents, which increased tensions and ultimately led to violence, were police actions in almost half the cases; police actions were "final" incidents before the outbreak of violence in 12 of the 24 surveyed disorders.

- No particular control tactic was successful in every situation. The varied effectiveness of control techniques emphasizes the need for advance training, planning, adequate intelligence systems, and knowledge of the ghetto community.

- Negotiations between Negroes—including young militants as well as older Negro leaders—and white officials concerning "terms of peace" occurred during virtually all the disorders surveyed. In many cases, these negotiations involved discussion of underlying grievances as well as the handling of the disorder by control authorities.

- The typical rioter was a teenager or young adult, a life-long resident of the city in which he rioted, a high school dropout; he was, nevertheless, somewhat better educated than his nonrioting Negro neighbor, and was usually underemployed or employed in a menial job. He was proud of his race, extremely hostile to both whites and middle-class Negroes and, although informed about politics, highly distrustful of the political system.

A Detroit survey revealed that approximately 11 percent of the total residents of two riot areas admitted participation in the rioting, 20 to 25 percent identified themselves as "bystanders," over 16 percent identified themselves as "counterrioters" who urged rioters to "cool it," and the remaining 48 to 53 percent said they were at home or elsewhere and did not participate. In a survey of Negro males between the ages of 15 and 35 residing in the disturbance area in Newark, about 45 percent identified themselves as rioters, and about 55 percent as "noninvolved."

- Most rioters were young Negro males. Nearly 53 percent of arrestees were between 15 and 24 years of age; nearly 81 percent between 15 and 35.

- In Detroit and Newark about 74 percent of the rioters were brought up in the North. In contrast, of the noninvolved, 36 percent in Detroit and 52 percent in Newark were brought up in the North.

- What the rioters appeared to be seeking was fuller participation in the social order and the material benefits enjoyed by the majority of

American citizens. Rather than rejecting the American system, they were anxious to obtain a place for themselves in it.

- Numerous Negro counterrioters walked the streets urging rioters to "cool it." The typical counterrioter was better educated and had higher income than either the rioter or the noninvolved.

- The proportion of Negroes in local government was substantially smaller than the Negro proportion of population. Only three of the 20 cities studied had more than one Negro legislator; none had ever had a Negro mayor or city manager. In only four cities did Negroes hold other important policy-making positions or serve as heads of municipal departments.

- Although almost all cities had some sort of formal grievance mechanism for handling citizen complaints, this typically was regarded by Negroes as ineffective and was generally ignored.

- Although specific grievances, varied from city to city, at least 12 deeply held grievances can be identified and ranked into three levels of relative intensity:

First level of intensity:

1. Police practices.
2. Unemployment and underemployment.
3. Inadequate housing.

Second level of intensity:

4. Inadequate education.
5. Poor recreation facilities and programs.
6. Ineffectiveness of the political structure and grievance mechanisms.

Third level of intensity:

7. Disrespectful white attitudes.
8. Discriminatory administration of justice.
9. Inadequacy of Federal programs.
10. Inadequacy of municipal services.
11. Discriminatory consumer and credit practices.
12. Inadequate welfare programs.

- The results of a three-city survey of various Federal programs—manpower, education, housing, welfare and community action—indicate that, despite substantial expenditures, the number of persons assisted constituted only a fraction of those in need.

The background of disorder is often as complex and difficult to analyze as the disorder itself. But we find that certain general conclusions can be drawn:

- Social and economic conditions in the riot cities constituted a clear pattern of severe disadvantage for Negroes compared with whites, whether the Negroes lived in the area where the riot took place or outside it. Negroes had completed fewer years of education and fewer had attended high school. Negroes were twice as likely to be unemployed and three times as likely to be in unskilled and service jobs. Negroes averaged 70 percent of the income earned by whites and were more than twice as likely to be living in poverty. Although housing cost Negroes relatively more, they had worse housing—three times as likely to be overcrowded and substandard. When compared to white suburbs, the relative disadvantage was even more pronounced.

A study of aftermath of disorder leads to disturbing conclusions. We find that, despite the institution of some postriot programs:

- Little basic change in the conditions underlying the outbreak of disorder has taken place. Actions to ameliorate Negro grievances have been limited and sporadic; with but few exceptions, they have not significantly reduced tensions.
- In several cities, the principal official response has been to train and equip the police with more sophisticated weapons.
- In several cities, increasing polarization is evident, with continuing breakdown of interracial communication, and growth of white segregationist or black separatist groups.

* * *

II. WHY DID IT HAPPEN?

Chapter 4.—The Basic Causes

In addressing the question "Why did it happen?" we shift our focus from the local to the national scene, from the particular events of the summer of 1967 to the factors within the society at large that created a mood of violence among many urban Negroes.

These factors are complex and interacting; they vary significantly in their effect from city to city and from year to year; and the consequences of one disorder, generating new grievances and new demands, become the causes of the next. Thus was created the "thicket of tension, conflicting evidence, and extreme opinions" cited by the President.

Despite these complexities, certain fundamental matters are clear. Of these, the most fundamental is the racial attitude and behavior of white Americans toward black Americans.

Race prejudice has shaped our history decisively; it now threatens to affect our future.

White racism is essentially responsible for the explosive mixture which has been accumulating in our cities since the end of World War II. Among the ingredients of this mixture are:

- *Pervasive discrimination and* segregation in employment, education, and housing, which have resulted in the continuing exclusion of great numbers of Negroes from the benefits of economic progress.

- *Black in-migration and white exodus,* which have produced the massive and growing concentrations of impoverished Negroes in our major cities, creating a growing crisis of deteriorating facilities and services and unmet human needs.

- *The black ghettos,* where segregation and poverty converge on the young to destroy opportunity and enforce failure. Crime, drug addiction, dependency on welfare, and bitterness and resentment against society in general and white society in particular are the result.

At the same time, most whites and some Negroes outside the ghetto have prospered to a degree unparalleled in the history of civilization. Through television and other media, this affluence has been flaunted before the eyes of the Negro poor and the jobless ghetto youth.

Yet these facts alone cannot be said to have caused the disorders. Recently, other powerful ingredients have begun to catalyze the mixture:

- *Frustrated hopes* are the residue of the unfulfilled expectations aroused by the great judicial and legislative victories of the civil rights movement and the dramatic struggle for equal rights in the South.

- *A climate that tends toward approval and encouragement of violence* as a form of protest has been created by white terrorism directed against nonviolent protest; by the open defiance of law and Federal authority by state and local officials resisting desegregation; and by some protest groups engaging in civil disobedience who turn their backs on nonviolence, go beyond the constitutionally protected rights of petition and free assembly, and resort to violence to attempt to compel alteration of laws and policies with which they disagree.

- *The frustrations of powerlessness* have led some Negroes to the conviction that there is no effective alternative to violence as a means of achieving redress of grievances, and of "moving the system." These frustrations are reflected in alienation and hostility toward the institutions of law and government and the white society which controls them, and in the reach toward racial consciousness and solidarity reflected in the slogan "Black Power."

- *A new mood* has sprung up among Negroes, particularly among the young, in which self-esteem and enhanced racial pride are replacing apathy and submission to "the system."

- *The police are not merely a "spark" factor.* To some Negroes police have come to symbolize white power, white racism, and white repression. And the fact is that many police do reflect and express these white attitudes. The atmosphere of hostility and cynicism is reinforced by a widespread belief among Negroes in the existence of police brutality and in a "double standard" of justice and protection—one for Negroes and one for whites.

* * *

To this point, we have attempted only to identify the prime components of the "explosive mixture." In the chapters that follow we seek to analyze them in the perspective of history. Their meaning, however, is clear:

In the summer of 1967, we have seen in our cities a chain reaction of racial violence. If we are heedless, none of us shall escape the consequences.

III. WHAT CAN BE DONE?

Chapter 12.—Control of Disorder

Preserving civil peace is the first responsibility of government. Unless the rule of law prevails, our society will lack not only order but also the environment essential to social and economic progress.

The maintenance of civil order cannot be left to the police alone. The police need guidance, as well as support, from mayors and other public officials. It is the responsibility of public officials to determine proper police policies, support adequate police standards for personnel and performance, and participate in planning for the control of disorders.

To maintain control of incidents which could lead to disorders, the Commission recommends that local officials:

- Assign seasoned, well-trained policemen and supervisory officers to patrol ghetto areas, and to respond to disturbances.

- Develop plans which will quickly muster maximum police manpower and highly qualified senior commanders at the outbreak of disorders.

- Provide special training in the prevention of disorders, and prepare police for riot control and for operation in units, with adequate command and control and field communication for proper discipline and effectiveness.
- Develop guidelines governing the use of control equipment and provide alternatives to the use of lethal weapons. Federal support for research in this area is needed.
- Establish an intelligence system to provide police and other public officials with reliable information that may help to prevent the outbreak of a disorder and to institute effective control measures in the event a riot erupts.
- Develop continuing contacts with ghetto residents to make use of the forces for order which exist within the community.
- Establish machinery for neutralizing rumors, and enabling Negro leaders and residents to obtain the facts. Create special rumor details to collect, evaluate, and dispel rumors that may lead to a civil disorder.

The Commission believes there is a grave danger that some communities may resort to the indiscriminate and excessive use of force. The harmful effects of over-reaction are incalculable. The Commission condemns moves to equip police departments with mass destruction weapons, such as automatic rifles, machine guns, and tanks. Weapons which are designed to destroy, not to control, have no place in densely populated urban communities.

The Commission recommends that the Federal Government share in the financing of programs for improvement of police forces, both in their normal law enforcement activities as well as in their response to civil disorders.

To assist government authorities in planning their response to civil disorder, this report contains a Supplement on Control of Disorder. It deals with specific problems encountered during riot control operations, and includes:

- Assessment of the present capabilities of police, National Guard and Army forces to control major riots, and recommendations for improvement.
- Recommended means by which the control operations of those forces may be coordinated with the response of other agencies, such as fire departments, and with the community at large.
- Recommendations for review and revision of Federal, state and local laws needed to provide the framework for control efforts and for the callup and interrelated action of public safety forces.

* * *

Chapter 15.—The News Media and the Disorders

In his charge to the Commission, the President asked: "What effect do the mass media have on the riots?"

The Commission determined that the answer to the President's question did not lie solely in the performance of the press and broadcasters in reporting the riots. Our analysis had to consider also the overall treatment by the media of the Negro ghettos, community relations, racial attitudes, and poverty—day by day and month by month, year in and year out.

A wide range of interviews with Government officials, law enforcement authorities, media personnel and other citizens, including ghetto residents, as well as a quantitative analysis of riot coverage and a special conference with industry representatives, leads us to conclude that:

- Despite instances of sensationalism, inaccuracy and distortion, newspapers, radio and television tried on the whole to give a balanced, factual account of the 1967 disorders.

- Elements of the news media failed to portray accurately the scale and character of the violence that occurred last summer. The overall effect was, we believe, an exaggeration of both mood and event.

- Important segments of the media failed to report adequately on the causes and consequences of civil disorders and on the underlying problems of race relations. They have not communicated to the majority of their audience—which is white—a sense of the degradation, misery, and hopelessness of life in the ghetto.

These failings must be corrected, and the improvement must come from within the industry. Freedom of the press is not the issue. Any effort to impose governmental restrictions would be inconsistent with fundamental constitutional precepts.

We have seen evidence that the news media are becoming aware of and concerned about their performance in this field. As that concern grows, coverage will improve. But much more must be done, and it must be done soon.

* * *

Chapter 16.—The Future of the Cities

By 1985, the Negro population in central cities is expected to increase by 68 percent to approximately 20.3 million. Coupled with the continued exodus of white families to the suburbs, this growth will produce majority Negro populations in many of the Nation's largest cities.

The future of these cities, and of their burgeoning Negro populations, is grim. Most new employment opportunities are being created in suburbs and outlying areas. This trend will continue unless important changes in public policy are made.

In prospect, therefore, is further deterioration of already inadequate municipal tax bases in the face of increasing demands for public services, and continuing unemployment and poverty among the urban Negro population:

Three choices are open to the Nation:

- We can maintain present policies continuing both the proportion of the Nation's resources now allocated to programs for the unemployed and the disadvantaged, and the inadequate and failing effort to achieve an integrated society.
- We can adopt a policy of "enrichment" aimed at improving dramatically the quality of ghetto life while abandoning integration as a goal.
- We can pursue integration by combining ghetto "enrichment" with policies which will encourage Negro movement out of central city areas.

The first choice, continuance of present policies, has ominous consequences for our society. The share of the Nation's resources now allocated to programs for the disadvantaged is insufficient to arrest the deterioration of life in central-city ghettos. Under such conditions, a rising proportion of Negroes may come to see in the deprivation and segregation they experience, a justification for violent protest, or for extending support to now isolated extremists who advocate civil disruption. Large-scale and continuing violence could result, followed by white retaliation and, ultimately, the separation of the two communities in a garrison state.

Even if violence does not occur, the consequences are unacceptable. Development of a racially integrated society, extraordinarily difficult today, will be virtually impossible when the present black central-city population of 12.1 million has grown to almost 21 million.

To continue present policies is to make permanent the division of our country into two societies: one, largely Negro and poor, located in the central cities: the other, predominantly white and affluent, located in the suburbs and in outlying areas.

The second choice, ghetto enrichment coupled with abandonment of integration, is also unacceptable. It is another way of choosing a permanently divided country. Moreover, equality cannot be achieved under conditions of nearly complete separation. In a country where the economy, and particularly the resources of employment, are predominantly white, a policy of separation can only relegate Negroes to a permanently inferior economic status.

We believe that the only possible choice for America is the third—a policy which combines ghetto enrichment with programs designed to encourage integration of substantial numbers of Negroes into the society outside the ghetto.

Enrichment must be an important adjunct to integration, for no matter how ambitious or energetic the program, few Negroes now living in central cities can be quickly integrated. In the meantime, large-scale improvement in the quality of ghetto life is essential.

But this can be no more than an interim strategy. Programs must be developed which will permit substantial Negro movement out of the ghettos. The primary goal must be a single society, in which every citizen will be free to live and work according to his capabilities and desires, not his color.

Chapter 17.—Recommendations for National Action

Introduction

No American—white or black—can escape the consequences of the continuing social and economic decay of our major cities.

Only a commitment to national action on an unprecedented scale can shape a future compatible with the historic ideals of American society.

The great productivity of our economy, and a Federal revenue system which is highly responsive to economic growth, can provide the resources.

The major need is to generate new will—the will to tax ourselves to the extent necessary to meet the vital needs of the Nation.

We have set forth goals and proposed strategies to reach those goals. We discuss and recommend programs not to commit each of us to specific parts of such programs, but to illustrate the type and dimension of action needed.

The major goal is the creation of a true union—a single society and a single American identity. Toward that goal, we propose the following objectives for national action:

- Opening up opportunities to those who are restricted by racial segregation and discrimination, and eliminating all barriers to their choice of jobs, education, and housing.
- Removing the frustration of powerlessness among the disadvantaged by providing the means for them to deal with the problems that affect their own lives and by increasing the capacity of our public and private institutions to respond to these problems.
- Increasing communication across racial lines to destroy stereotypes, halt polarization, end distrust and hostility, and create common ground for efforts toward public order and social justice.

We propose these aims to fulfill our pledge of equality and to meet the fundamental needs of a democratic and civilized society—domestic peace and social justice.

Employment

Pervasive unemployment and underemployment are the most persistent and serious grievances in minority areas. They are inextricably linked to the problem of civil disorder.

Despite growing Federal expenditures for manpower development and training programs, and sustained general economic prosperity and increasing demands for skilled workers, about 2 million—white and non-white—are permanently unemployed. About 10 million are underemployed, of whom 6.5 million work full time for wages below the poverty line.

The 500,000 "hard-core" unemployed in the central cities who lack a basic education and are unable to hold a steady job are made up in large part of Negro males between the ages of 18 and 25. In the riot cities which we surveyed, Negroes were three times as likely as whites to hold unskilled jobs, which are often part time, seasonal, low paying and "dead end."

Negro males between the ages of 15 and 25 predominated among the rioters. More than 20 percent of the rioters were unemployed, and many who were employed held intermittent, low status, unskilled jobs which they regarded as below their education and ability.

The Commission recommends that the Federal Government:

- Undertake joint efforts with cities and states to consolidate existing manpower programs to avoid fragmentation and duplication.
- Take immediate action to create 2 million new jobs over the next 3 years—1 million in the public sector and 1 million in the private sector—to absorb the hard-core unemployed and materially reduce the level of underemployment for all workers, black and white. We propose 250,000 public sector and 300,000 private sector jobs in the first year.
- Provide on-the-job training by both public and private employers with reimbursement to private employers for the extra costs of training the hard-core unemployed, by contract or by tax credits.
- Provide tax and other incentives to investment in rural as well as urban poverty areas in order to offer to the rural poor an alternative to migration to urban centers.
- Take new and vigorous action to remove artificial barriers to employment and promotion, including not only racial discrimination but, in certain cases, arrest records or lack of a high school diploma. Strengthen those agencies such as the Equal Employment Opportunity Commission, charged with eliminating discriminatory practices, and provide full support for Title VI of the 1964 Civil Rights Act allowing Federal grant-in-aid funds to be withheld from activities which discriminate on grounds of color or race.

The Commission commends the recent public commitment of the National Council of the Building and Construction Trades Unions, **AFL-CIO**, to encourage and recruit Negro membership in apprenticeship programs. This commitment should be intensified and implemented.

The **AFL-CIO** was the largest federation of labor unions in the U.S.

Education

Education in a democratic society must equip children to develop their potential and to participate fully in American life. For the community at large, the schools have discharged this responsibility well. But for many minorities, and particularly for the children of the ghetto, the schools have failed to provide the educational experience which could overcome the effects of discrimination and deprivation.

This failure is one of the persistent sources of grievance and resentment within the Negro community. The hostility of Negro parents and students toward the school system is generating increasing conflict and causing disruption within many city school districts. But the most dramatic evidence of the relationship between educational practices and civil disorders lies in the high incidence of riot participation by ghetto youth who have not completed high school.

The bleak record of public education for ghetto children is growing worse. In the critical skills—verbal and reading ability—Negro students are falling further behind whites with each year of school completed. The high unemployment and underemployment rate for Negro youth is evidence, in part, of the growing educational crisis.

We support integration as the priority education strategy; it is essential to the future of American society. In this last summer's disorders we have seen the consequences of racial isolation at all levels, and of attitudes toward race, on both sides, produced by three centuries of myth, ignorance, and bias. It is indispensable that opportunities for interaction between the races be expanded.

We recognize that the growing dominance of pupils from disadvantaged minorities in city school populations will not soon be reversed. No matter how great the effort toward desegregation, many children of the ghetto will not, within their school careers, attend integrated schools.

If existing disadvantages are not to be perpetuated, we must drastically improve the quality of ghetto education. Equality of results with all-white schools must be the goal.

* * *

The Welfare System

Our present system of public welfare is designed to save money instead of people, and tragically ends up doing neither. This system has two critical deficiencies:

First, it excludes large numbers of persons who are in great need, and who, if provided a decent level of support, might be able to become more productive and self-sufficient. No Federal funds are available for millions of unemployed and underemployed men and women who are needy but neither aged, handicapped nor the parents of minor children.

Second, for those included, the system provides assistance well below the minimum necessary for a decent level of existence, and imposes restrictions that encourage continued dependency on welfare and undermine self-respect.

A welter of statutory requirements and administrative practices and regulations operate to remind recipients that they are considered untrustworthy, promiscuous, and lazy. Residence requirements prevent assistance to people in need who are newly arrived in the state. Searches of recipients' homes violate privacy. Inadequate social services compound the problems.

* * *

Housing

After more than three decades of fragmented and grossly underfunded Federal housing programs, nearly 6 million substandard housing units remain occupied in the United States.

The housing problem is particularly acute in the minority ghettos. Nearly two-thirds of all nonwhite families living in the central cities today live in neighborhoods marked by substandard housing and general urban blight. [. . .]

* * *

Conclusion

One of the first witnesses to be invited to appear before this Commission was Dr. Kenneth B. Clark, a distinguished and perceptive scholar. Referring to the reports of earlier riot commissions, he said:

> I read that report [. . .] of the 1919 riot in Chicago, and it is as if I were reading the report of the investigating committee on the Harlem riot of '35, the report of the investigating committee on the Harlem riot of '43, the report of the McCone Commission on the Watts riot.
>
> I must again in candor say to you members of this Commission—it is a kind of Alice in Wonderland—with the same moving picture reshown over and over again, the same analysis, the same recommendations, and the same inaction.

These words come to our minds as we conclude this report.

We have provided an honest beginning. We have learned much. But we have uncovered no startling truths, no unique insights, no simple solutions. The destruction and the bitterness of racial disorder, the harsh polemics of black revolt and white repression have been seen and heard before in this country.

It is time now to end the destruction and the violence, not only in the streets of the ghetto but in the lives of people.

* * *

THE NEWS MEDIA AND THE DISORDERS

The President's charge to the Commission asked specifically: "What effect do the mass media have on the riots?"

The question is far reaching, and a sure answer is beyond the range of presently available scientific techniques. Our conclusions and recommendations are based upon subjective as well as objective factors; interviews as well as statistics; isolated examples as well as general trends.

Freedom of the press is not the issue. A free press is indispensable to the preservation of the other freedoms this Nation cherishes. The recommendations in this chapter have thus been developed under the strong conviction that only a press unhindered by government can contribute to freedom.

To answer the President's question, the Commission:

- Directed its field survey teams to question government officials, law enforcement agents, media personnel, and ordinary citizens about their attitudes and reactions to reporting of the riots.

- Arranged for interviews of media representatives about their coverage of the riots.

- Conducted special interviews with ghetto residents about their response to coverage.

- Arranged for a quantitative analysis of the content of television programs and newspaper reporting in 15 riot cities during the period of the disorder and the days immediately before and after.

- From November 10–12, 1967, sponsored and participated in a conference of representatives from all levels of the newspaper, news magazine, and broadcasting industries at Poughkeepsie, N.Y.

Finally, of course, the Commissioners read newspapers, listened to the radio, watched television, and thus formed their own impressions of media coverage. All of these data, impressions, and attitudes provide the foundation for our conclusions.

The Commission also determined, very early, that the answer to the President's question did not lie solely in the performance of the press and broadcasters in reporting the riots proper. Our analysis had to consider also the overall treatment by the media of the Negro ghettos, community relations, racial attitudes, urban and rural poverty—day by day and month by month, year in and year out.

On this basis, we have reached three conclusions:

First, that despite instances of sensationalism, inaccuracies, and distortions, newspapers, radio, and television, on the whole, made a real effort to give a balanced, factual account of the 1967 disorders.

Second, that despite this effort, the portrayal of the violence that occurred last summer failed to reflect accurately its scale and character. The overall effect was, we believe, an exaggeration of both mood and event.

Third, and ultimately most important, we believe that the media have thus far failed to report adequately on the causes and consequences of civil disorders and the underlying problems of race relations.

With these comments as a perspective, we discuss first the coverage of last summer's disturbances. We will then summarize our concerns with overall coverage of race relations.

Coverage of the 1967 Disturbances

We have found a significant imbalance between what actually happened in our cities and what the newspaper, radio, and television coverage of the riots told us happened. The Commission, in studying last summer's disturbances, visited many of the cities and interviewed participants and observers. We found that the disorders, as serious as they were, were less destructive, less widespread, and less of a black-white confrontation than most people believed.

Lacking other sources of information, we formed our original impressions and beliefs from what we saw on television, heard on the radio, and read in newspapers and magazines. We are deeply concerned that millions of other Americans, who must rely on the mass media, likewise formed incorrect impressions and judgments about what went on in many American cities last summer.

As we started to probe the reasons for this imbalance between reality and impression, we first believed that the media had sensationalized the disturbances, consistently overplaying violence and giving disproportionate amounts of time to emotional events and militant leaders. To test this theory, we commissioned a systematic, quantitative analysis, covering the content of newspaper and television reporting in 15 cities where disorders occurred. The results of this analysis do not support our early belief. Of 955 television sequences of riot and racial news examined, 837 could be classified for predominant atmosphere as either "emotional," "calm," or "normal." Of these, 494 were classified as calm, 262 as emotional, and 81 as normal. Only a small proportion of all scenes analyzed showed actual mob action, people looting, sniping, setting fires, or being injured, or killed. Moderate Negro leaders were shown more frequently than militant leaders on television news broadcasts.

Of 3,779 newspaper articles analyzed, more focused on legislation which should be sought and planning which should be done to control ongoing riots and prevent future riots than on any other topic. The findings of this analysis are explained in detail later in this chapter. They make it clear that the imbalance between actual events and the portrayal of those events in the press and on the air cannot be attributed solely to sensationalism in reporting and presentation.

We have, however, identified several factors which, it seems to us, did work to create incorrect and exaggerated impressions about the scope and intensity of the disorders.

First, despite the overall statistical picture, there were instances of gross flaws in presenting news of the 1967 riots. Some newspapers printed scare headlines unsupported by the mild stories that followed. All media reported rumors that had no basis in fact. Some newsmen staged riot events for the cameras. Examples are included in the next section.

Second, the press obtained much factual information about the scale of the disorders—property damage, personal injury, and deaths—from local officials, who often were inexperienced in dealing with civil disorders and not always able to sort out fact from rumor in the confusion. At the height of the Detroit riot, some news reports of property damage put the figure in excess of $500 million. Subsequent investigation shows it to be $40 to $45 million. The initial estimates were not the independent judgment of reporters or editors. They came from beleaguered government officials. But the news media gave currency to these errors. Reporters uncritically accepted, and editors uncritically published, the inflated figures, leaving an indelible impression of damage up to more than 10 times greater than actually occurred.

Third, the coverage of the disorders—particularly on television—tended to define the events as black-white confrontations. In fact, almost all of the deaths, injuries, and property damage occurred in all-Negro neighborhoods, and thus the disorders were not "race riots" as that term is generally understood.

Closely linked to these problems is the phenomenon of cumulative effect. As the summer of 1967 progressed, we think Americans often began to associate more or less neutral sights and sounds (like a squad car with flashing red lights, a burning building, a suspect in police custody) with racial disorders, so that the appearance of any particular item, itself hardly inflammatory, set off a whole sequence of association with riot events. Moreover, the summer's news was not seen and heard in isolation. Events of these past few years—the Watts riot, other disorders, and the growing momentum of the civil rights movement—conditioned the responses of readers and viewers and heightened their reactions. What the public saw and read last summer thus produced emotional reactions and left vivid impressions not wholly attributable to the material itself.

Fear and apprehension of racial unrest and violence are deeply rooted in American society. They color and intensify reactions to news of racial trouble and threats of racial conflict. Those who report and disseminate news must be conscious of the background of anxieties and apprehension against which their stories are projected. This does not mean that the media should manage the news or tell less than the truth. Indeed, we believe that it would be imprudent and even dangerous to downplay coverage in the hope that censored reporting of inflammatory incidents somehow will diminish violence. Once a disturbance occurs, the word will spread independently of newspapers and television. To attempt to ignore these events or portray them as something other than what they are can only diminish confidence in the media and increase the effectiveness of those who monger rumors and the fears of those who listen.

But to be complete, the coverage must be representative. We suggest that the main failure of the media last summer was that the totality of its coverage was not as representative as it should have been to be accurate. We believe that to live up to their own professed standards, the media simply must exercise a higher degree of care and a greater level of sophistication than they have yet shown in this area—higher, perhaps, than the level ordinarily acceptable with other stories.

This is not "just another story." It should not be treated like one. Admittedly, some of what disturbs us about riot coverage last summer stems from circumstances beyond media control. But many of the inaccuracies of fact, tone, and mood were due to the failure of reporters and editors to ask tough enough questions about official reports and to apply the most rigorous standards possible in evaluating and presenting the news. Reporters and editors must be sure that descriptions and pictures of violence, and emotional or inflammatory sequences or articles, even though "true" in isolation, are really representative and do not convey an impression at odds with the overall reality of events. The media too often did not achieve this level of sophisticated, skeptical, careful news judgment during last summer's riots.

The Media and Race Relations

Our second and fundamental criticism is that the news media have failed to analyze and report adequately on racial problems in the United States and, as a related matter, to meet the Negro's legitimate expectations in journalism. By and large, news organizations have failed to communicate to both their black and white audiences a sense of the problems America faces and the sources of potential solutions. The media report and write from the standpoint of a white man's world. The ills of the ghetto, the difficulties of life there, the Negro's burning sense of grievance, are seldom conveyed. Slights and indignities are part of the Negro's daily life, and many of them come from what he now calls the "white press"—a press that repeatedly, if unconsciously, reflects the biases, the paternalism, the indifference of white America. This may be understandable, but it is not excusable in an institution that has the mission to inform and educate the whole of our society.

ROBERT KENNEDY

"Book and Author Luncheon," February 8, 1968

In this address presented in the wake of the Tet offensive, a shockingly broad and determined succession of attacks by communist forces in South Vietnam, Kennedy described a series of "illusions" that undermined the war effort in Vietnam. He followed up with a set of "basic truths" that he thought should inform U.S. policy going forward.

SOURCE: *"Address by Senator Robert F. Kennedy, Book and Author Luncheon, Chicago, Ill., February 8, 1968."* Congressional Record, *vol. 114, part 3, U.S. Government Printing Office, 1968, pp. 2671–2672.*

The events of the last few weeks have demonstrated anew the truth of Lord Halifax's dictum that although hope "is very good company by the way ... [it] is generally a wrong guide."

Our enemy, savagely striking at will across all of South Vietnam, has finally shattered the mask of official illusion with which we have concealed our true circumstances, even from ourselves. But a short time ago we were serene in our reports and predictions of progress. In April, our commanding general told us that "the South Vietnamese are fighting now better than ever before ... their record in combat ... reveals an exceptional performance." In August, another general told us that "the really big battles of the Vietnam war are over ... the enemy has been so badly pummeled he'll never give us trouble again." In December, we were told that we were winning "battle after battle," that "the secure proportion of the population has grown from about 45 percent to 65 percent and in the contested areas the tide continues to run with us."

Those dreams are gone. The Vietcong will probably withdraw from the cities, as they were forced to withdraw from the American Embassy. Thousands of them will be dead. But they will, nevertheless, have demonstrated that no part or person of South Vietnam, is secure from their attacks: neither district capitals nor American bases, neither the peasant in his rice paddy nor the commanding general of our own great forces.

No one can predict the exact shape or outcome of the battles now in progress, in **Saigon** or at Khesahn. Let us pray that we will succeed at the lowest possible cost to our young men. But whatever their outcome, the events of the last two weeks have taught us something. For the sake of those young Americans who are fighting today, if for no other reason, the time has come to take a new look at the war in Vietnam; not by cursing the past but by using it to illuminate the future. And the first and necessary step is to face the facts. It is to seek out the austere and painful reality of Vietnam, freed from wishful thinking, false hopes and sentimental dreams. It is to rid ourselves of the "good company" of those illusions which have lured us into the deepening swamp of Vietnam. "If you would guide by the light of reason," said Holmes, "you must let your mind be bold." We will find no guide to the future in Vietnam unless we are bold enough to confront the grim anguish, the reality, of that battlefield which was once a nation called South Vietnam, stripped of deceptive illusions. It is time for the truth.

Saigon was the capital of the U.S.-backed government of South Vietnam. It is now Ho Chi Minh City.

We must, first of all, rid ourselves of the illusion that the events of the past two weeks represent some sort of victory. That is not so.

It is said the Vietcong will not be able to hold the cities. This is probably true. But they have demonstrated despite all our reports of progress, of government strength and enemy weakness, that half a million American soldiers with 700,000 Vietnamese allies, with total command of the air, total command of the sea, backed by huge resources and the most modern weapons, are unable to secure even a single city from the attacks of an enemy whose total strength is about 250,000. It is as if James Madison were able to claim a great victory in 1812 because the British only burned Washington instead of annexing it to the British Empire.

We are told that the enemy suffered terrible losses; and there is no doubt he did. They cannot, however, be as devastating as the figures appear. The Secretary of Defense has told us that "during all of 1967 the Communists lost about 165,000 effectives," yet enemy main force strength "has been maintained at a relatively constant level of about 110,000–115,000 during the past year." Thus it would seem that no matter how many Vietcong and North Vietnamese we claim to kill, through some miraculous effort of will, enemy strength remains the same. Now our intelligence chief tells us that of 60,000 men thrown into the attacks on the cities, 20,000 have been killed. If only two men have been seriously wounded for everyone dead—a very conservative estimate—the entire enemy force has been put out of action. Who, then, is doing the fighting?

Again it is claimed that the Communists expected a large-scale popular uprising which did not occur. How ironic it is that we should claim a victory because a people whom we have given sixteen thousand lives, billions of dollars and almost a decade to defend, did not rise in arms against us. More disillusioning and painful is the fact the population did not rise to defend its freedom against the Vietcong. Thousands of men and arms were infiltrated into populated urban areas over a period of days, if not of weeks. Yet few, if any, citizens rushed to inform their protectors of this massive infiltration. At best they simply shut their doors to concern, waiting for others to resolve the issue. Did we know the attack was coming? If so, why did we not strike first, and where were the forces needed for effective defense?

For years we have been told that the measure of our success and progress in Vietnam was increasing security and control for the population. Now we have seen that none of the population is secure and no area is under sure control. Four years ago when we only had about 30,000 troops in Vietnam, the Vietcong were unable to amount the assaults on cities they have now conducted against our enormous forces. At one time a suggestion that we protect enclaves was derided. Now there are no protected enclaves.

This has not happened because our men are not brave or effective, because they are. It is because we have misconceived the nature of the war: it is because we have sought to resolve by military might a conflict whose issue depends upon the will and conviction of the South Vietnamese people. It is like sending a lion to halt an epidemic of jungle rot.

This misconception rests on a second illusion—the illusion that we can win a war which the South Vietnamese cannot win for themselves.

Two Presidents and countless officials have told us for seven years that although we can help the South Vietnamese, it is their war and they must win it; as Secretary of Defense McNamara told us last month, "We cannot provide the South Vietnamese with the will to survive as an independent nation ... or with the ability and self-discipline a people must have to govern themselves. These qualities and attributes are essential contributions to the struggle only the South Vietnamese can supply." Yet this wise and certain counsel has gradually become an empty slogan, as mounting frustration has led us to transform the war into an American military effort.

The South Vietnamese Senate, with only one dissenting vote, refuses to draft 18 and 19 year old South Vietnamese, with a member of the Assembly asking "why should Vietnamese boys be sent to die for Americans."—While 19 year old American boys fight to maintain this Senate and Assembly in Saigon. Every detached observer has testified to the enormous corruption which pervades every level of South Vietnamese official life. Hundreds of millions of dollars are stolen by private individuals and government officials while the American people are being asked to pay higher taxes to finance our assistance effort. Despite continual promises the Saigon regime refuses to act against corruption. Late last year, after all our pressure for reform, two high army officers were finally dismissed for "criminal" corruption. Last month, these same two officers were given new and powerful commands. In the meantime, incorruptible officers resign out of frustration and defeat.

Perhaps, we could live with corruption and inefficiency by themselves. However the consequence is not simply the loss of money or of popular confidence; it is the loss of American lives. For government corruption is the source of the enemy's strength. It is, more than anything else, the reason why the greatest power on earth cannot defeat a tiny and primitive foe.

You cannot expect people to risk their lives and endure hardship unless they have a stake in their own society. They must have a clear sense of identification with their own government, a belief they are participating in a cause worth fighting for. Political and economic reform are not simply idealistic slogans or noble goals to be postponed until the fighting is over. They are the principal weapons of battle. People will not fight to line the pockets of generals or swell the bank accounts of the wealthy. They are far more likely to close their eyes and shut their doors in the face of their government—even as they did last week.

More than any election, more than any proud boasts, that single fact reveals the truth. We have an ally in name only. We support a government without supporters. Without the efforts of American arms that government would not last a day.

The third illusion is that the unswerving pursuit of military victory, whatever its cost, is in the interest of either ourselves or the people of Vietnam. For the people of Vietnam, the last three years have meant little but horror. Their tiny land has been devastated by a weight of bombs and shells greater than Nazi Germany knew in the Second World War. We have dropped twelve tons of bombs for every square mile in North and South Vietnam. Whole provinces have been substantially destroyed. More than two million South Vietnamese are now homeless refugees. Imagine the impact in our own country if an equivalent number—over 25 million Americans—were wandering homeless or interned in refugee camps, and millions more refugees were being created as New York and Chicago, Washington and

Boston, were being destroyed by a war raging in their streets. Whatever the outcome of these battles, it is the people we seek to defend who are the greatest losers.

Nor does it serve the interests of America to fight this war as if moral standards could be subordinated to immediate necessities. Last week, a Vietcong suspect was turned over to the Chief of the Vietnamese Security Services, who executed him on the spot—a flat violation of the Geneva Convention on the Rules of War. Of course, the enemy is brutal and cruel, and has done the same thing many times. But we are not fighting the Communists in order to become more like them—we fight to preserve our differences. Moreover, such actions—like the widespread use of artillery and air power in the centers of cities—may hurt us far more in the long run than it helps today. The photograph of the execution was on front pages all around the world—leading our best and oldest friends to ask, more in sorrow than in anger, what has happened to America?

The fourth illusion is that the American national interest is identical with—or should be subordinated to—the selfish interest of an incompetent military regime. We are told, of course, that the battle for South Vietnam is in reality a struggle for 250 million Asians—the beginning of a Great Society for all of Asia. But this is pretension. We can and should offer reasonable assistance to Asia; but we cannot build a Great Society there if we cannot build one in our own country. We cannot speak extravagantly of a struggle for 250 million Asians, when a struggle for 15 million in one Asian country so strains our forces, that another Asian country, a fourth-rate power which we have already once defeated in battle, dares to seize an American ship and hold and humiliate her crew.

And we are told that the war in Vietnam will settle the future course of Asia. But that is a prayerful wish based on unsound hope, meant only to justify the enormous sacrifices we have already made. The truth is that Communism triumphed in China twenty years ago, and was extended to Tibet. It lost in Malaya and the Philippines, met disaster in Indonesia, and was fought to a standstill in Korea. It has struggled against governments in Burma for twenty years without success, and it may struggle in Thailand for many more. The outcome in each country depends and will depend on the intrinsic strength of the government, the particular circumstances of the country, and the particular character of the insurgent movement. The truth is that the war in Vietnam does not promise the end of all threats to Asia and ultimately to the United States; rather, if we proceed on our present course, it promises only years and decades of further draining conflict on the mainland of Asia—conflict which, as our finest military leaders have always warned, could lead us only to national tragedy.

There is an American interest in South Vietnam. We have an interest in maintaining the strength of our commitments—and surely we have demonstrated that. With all the lives and resources we have poured into Vietnam, is there anyone to argue that a government with any support from its people, with any competence to rule, with any determination to defend itself, would not long ago have been victorious over any insurgent movement, however assisted from outside its borders?

And we have another, more immediate interest: to protect the lives of our gallant young men, and to conserve American resources. But we do not have an interest in the survival of a privileged class, growing ever more wealthy from the corruption of war, which after all our sacrifices on their behalf, can ask why Vietnamese boys should die for Americans.

The fifth illusion is that this war can be settled in our own way and in our own time on our own terms. Such a settlement is the privilege of the triumphant; of those who crush their enemies in battle or wear away their will to fight.

We have not done this, nor is there any prospect we will achieve such a victory.

For twenty years, first the French and then the United States, have been predicting victory in Vietnam. In 1961 and 1962, as well as 1966 and 1967, we have been told that "the tide is turning"; "there is 'light at the end of the tunnel'," "we can soon bring home the troops—victory is near—, the enemy is tiring." Once, in 1962, I participated in such predictions myself. But for twenty years we have been wrong. The history of conflict among nations does not record another such lengthy and consistent chronicle of error. It is time to discard so proven a fallacy and face the reality that a military victory is not in sight, and that it probably will never come.

Unable to defeat our enemy or break his will—at least without a huge, long, and ever more costly effort—we must actively seek a peaceful settlement. We can no longer harden our terms everywhere Hanoi indicates it may be prepared to negotiate; and we must be willing to foresee a settlement which will give the Vietcong a chance to participate in the political life of the country. Not because we want them to, but because that is the only way in which this struggle can be settled. No one knows if negotiations will bring a peaceful settlement, but we do know there will be no peaceful settlement without negotiations. Nor can we have these negotiations just on our own terms. We may have to make concessions and take risks, and surely we will have to negotiate directly with the NLF[1] as well as Hanoi. Surely it is only another illusion that still denies this basic necessity. What we must not do is confuse the prestige staked on a particular policy with the interest of the United States; nor should we be unwilling to take risks for peace when we are willing to risk so many lives in war.

A year ago, when our adversary offered negotiations if only we would halt the bombing of the North, we replied with a demand for his virtual surrender. Officials at the highest level of our government felt that we were on the edge of a military victory and negotiations, except on our terms, were not necessary. Now, a year too late, we have set fewer conditions for a bombing halt, conditions which

---

1. In a break with the Johnson administration, Kennedy advocated direct talks with the NLF as well as the communist government of North Vietnam. The NLF, or National Liberation Front, was the communist insurgency in South Vietnam, better known as the Vietcong.

clearly would have been more acceptable then. And the intervening year, for all its terrible costs, the deaths of thousands of Americans and South Vietnamese, has not improved our position in the least. When the chance for negotiations comes again, let us not postpone for another year the recognition of what is really possible and necessary to a peaceful settlement.

These are some of the illusions which must be discarded if the events of last week are to prove not simply a tragedy, but a lesson: a lesson which carries with it some basic truths.

First, that a total military victory is not within sight or around the corner; that, in fact, it is probably beyond our grasp; and that the effort to win such a victory will only result in the further slaughter of thousands of innocent and helpless people—a slaughter which will forever rest on our national conscience.

Second, that the pursuit of such a victory is not necessary to our national interest and is even damaging that interest.

Third, that the progress we have claimed toward increasing our control over the country and the security of the population is largely illusory.

Fourth, that the central battle in this war cannot be measured by body counts or bomb damage, but by the extent to which the people of South Vietnam act on a sense of common purpose and hope with those that govern them.

Fifth, that the current regime in Saigon is unwilling or incapable of being an effective ally in the war against the Communists.

Sixth, that a political compromise is not just the best path to peace, but the only path, and we must show as much willingness to risk some of our prestige for peace as to risk the lives of young men in war.

Seventh, that the escalation policy in Vietnam, far from strengthening and consolidating international resistance to aggression, is injuring our country through the world, reducing the faith of other peoples in our wisdom and purpose and weakening the world's resolve to stand together for freedom and strength.

Eighth, that the best way to save our most precious stake in Vietnam—the lives of our soldiers—is to stop the enlargement of the war, and that the best way to end casualties is to end the war.

Ninth, that our nation must be told the truth about this war, in all its terrible reality, both because it is right—and because only in this way can any administration rally the public conscience and unity for the shadowed days which lie ahead.

No war has ever demanded more bravery from our people and our government—not just bravery under fire or the bravery to make sacrifices—but the bravery to discard the comfort of illusion—to do away with false hopes and alluring promises. Reality is grim and painful. But it is only a remote echo of the anguish toward which a policy founded on illusion is surely taking us. This is a great nation and a strong people. Any who seek to comfort rather than speak plainly, reassure rather than instruct, promise satisfaction rather than reveal frustration—they deny that greatness and drain that strength. For today as it was in the beginning, it is the truth that makes us free.

DAVID HARRIS

"The Assumptions of the Draft," 1968

Harris participated in the Student Non-Violent Coordinating Committee's "Mississippi Summer" voter registration drive in 1966. In 1967, he launched the Resistance, an anti-draft organization. When Harris received his draft notice, he was arrested, convicted of draft evasion, and sentenced to fifteen months in federal prison. In August 1968, the Military Selective Service Act of 1967 was in force. It granted student deferments, but ended them upon completion of a four-year degree or a twenty-fourth birthday. When men completed their registration, they received a "draft card."

SOURCE: *Mitchell Goodman,* The Movement toward a New America: The Beginnings of a Long Revolution; (A Collage) A What? *Knopf, 1970, pp. 445–446. I have silently corrected spelling errors.*

I'd like to talk about the basic assumptions which that system represents, and the pillars upon which it is built, because I think you and I have to understand what it means to carry a draft card. One of the things it means is a set of terms you accept, and for a moment I'd like to lay those terms out.

I. The most obvious assumption of military conscription is that the lives of young people in this country belong not to those young people; the lives of those young people instead are possessions of the state, to be used by the state when and where the state chooses to use them. The decisions made by those young people are not decisions made on the terms that they find in their lives. They are rather decisions that are made on the terms of the state because those people belong to the state. What the draft card represents is a pledge. It's a pledge that all of you have signed to the American state. That pledge says, *"When and where you decide murder to be a fit international policy, I'm your boy."*

If your relationship to the state is one of subserviance, then you can expect that state to reproduce that subserviance in kind around the world. History should leave us no doubt about that. And what we see happening in a situation like Vietnam today is not a mistake. It is not something that's fallen down out of the sky on all of us. Rather, we see the American logic coming to fruition. We see a dispossessed people dispossessing other people of their lives.

The first problem that you and I face is the problem of repossessing that basic instrument called a life. That life all of you have signed over to the state. And it is only when we begin to repossess those lives that you and I can ever talk about those lives having meaning or about living in a society that was really shaped by the meaning of those lives.

II. The second assumption of conscription is perhaps the least obvious, but it is also the most important. For a moment, I'd like all of you to think of your draft cards as an educational mechanism. You're given a draft card to teach you a way of thinking about yourself and a way of thinking about people around you. And what has been taught to a generation of young people in this country by conscription is a basic fact that has to do with a mode of energy of life.

You know for all of us there are thousands, literally thousands of psychological and emotional resources one might go to to find the energy to pursue one's life from day to day. But rather than any of those various energies, what we live in is one of those energies organized. *And what that draft card has taught people from day to day to day in their lives is how consistently to live under the auspices of fear.* How continually when they seek those resources that one needs to live a life, how continually to go to fear for those. And as you and I look around us, we can say that fear is not just a simple, personal, psychological fact; what you and I live in the midst of is the organized politics of fear.

If we were to dispense with words like "left" and "right," which may be totally inadequate to understand those organizations from the point of view of what human energy is, their base for social organization, what model of man are they based upon, then what you and I can say in the world today is that we live in the unanimous organized politics of fear. That fear has made men blind. That blindness has made people starve. That blindness is the fact of lives around the world today.

What you and I can reasonably do, then, is not say that we won't be afraid, because I've never met a man who wasn't afraid. What you and I can say is that we refuse to make that fear the central fact of our lives. We refuse to make it the hub around which we revolve.

Most of all, we refuse to build that fear into social organizations. What we can say is, we may be afraid, but that fear will not be imposed by us on the people around us. That fear will not be made into a society, which means that no longer can we continue to act under the auspices of that fear. And what we in the Resistance have done is said: NO MORE. No more will we breed and extend that fear. No more will we be that fear's servant.

III. The third assumption of conscription is the most obvious: that is, 80% of the people in the world today live lives that we could characterize as miserable. They live those lives not because the world does not possess the resources to give them meaningful lives. You live in a country that every hour spends seven million dollars on weapons. Every month we spend the money for armaments for the war in Vietnam that is necessary to feed every starving person in the world today. The world is not lacking the sustenance for those people.

Rather, what stands between those people and anything we might understand as the basic refinements of life is you and me, and the fact that you and I and the people around the world have made the decision that it's much more important to kill those people, that it's much more important to see every starving face in the world today as a potential enemy than it is to go to those people and talk to their hunger and give them food.

And if we are to ask ourselves what institution in this society stands as a representative of that decision, what we can say is that the United States military is the obvious representative of that decision on your and my parts, and that the United States military does not exist without conscription, and conscription does not exist without you and me. That system of conscription is not General Hershey. It is not Lyndon Johnson. It is not any Congressman or Senator who voted upon that bill. It is not any one of the little old ladies that shuffle the daily papers of the **SSS**. Military conscription is every man that carries a draft card.

The **SSS**, or Selective Service System, was the arm of the federal bureaucracy that ran the draft.

You and I are the bricks and mortar of that system. And the most elaborate bureaucracy for selective service in the world does not function without people such as you and me willing to sign our lives over to that system. Without you and me, it's nothing. I mean, the beautiful thing about American totalitarianism is that it is participatory. Which means that if you don't buy it, it doesn't move. And I don't buy it.

I think you buy it when you carry a draft card. I think you become one more link in a whole chain of death and oppression on people's lives around the world.

What we in the Resistance have said about that act of refusing to cooperate with military conscription is not that we see it as a final act, not that we see it even as the great culmination. It's one little thing. It's one step. But it's the first step. To take that step means for most of you taking on what's probably going to be a wholly new social role. That's called the role of criminal. . .

You and I have to stand up. The first way you can stand up is to take that little piece of white paper called a draft card that you carry around in your pocket, you can take it and say:

IN REALITY, THIS IS NOT A PIECE OF WHITE PAPER. IN REALITY, THIS IS A DEATH WARRANT. I'VE SIGNED THIS DEATH WARRANT, AND I NOW TEAR THIS DEATH WARRANT UP. MY NAME GOES OUT ON NO MORE DEATH WARRANTS, AND MY BODY STANDS BETWEEN ANY MAN AND THAT DEATH WARRANT. I STAND HERE TODAY AND TOMORROW AND THE NEXT DAY WITH MY BROTHERS AND I DON'T STOP STANDING UNTIL ALL MY BROTHERS ARE ON THEIR FEET.

AKMED LORENCE

Transcript, 1967

Akmed Lorence was a Vietnam veteran who was interviewed in 1967 for the documentary No Vietnamese Ever Called Me Nigger, *which explored the black antiwar movement in New York City. This document is a transcript of all his comments during the film. Different scenes are divided by asterisks.*

SOURCE: No Vietnamese Ever Called Me Nigger, *directed by David Loeb Weiss. 1968; Cinema Guild, 2005. DVD. Transcription by Linda Sinclair.*

I had a friend, right, he was a honk. Came from DC; came from a rich DC family. Lives in Georgetown. His father's president of RCA in Washington DC and this guy had been to pretty decent schools, the best schools. It so happened that—I don't know if it was his luck or his bad luck but he ended up humping a radio with me. Humping a radio, you know, carrying a radio on your back, with me.

Now, I told him that America was corrupt, the system was bad, and that all whites hated any kind of colored people. And he told me, "you're a racist. You're sick, man."

I told him you watch your people for one month and you tell me whether they are racist or not. About a month and a half later he came to me, and he told me, "Lorence," he said, "I'm a man without a country."

So I said to him, I says, "why are you kidding me? Are you pulling a fast one on me again?"

He said, "no man, I'm a man without a country."

I said, "why?"

He said, "I'll tell you later." Later on he came over to me and he ran it down to me. He said, "you were right." He says, "I watched them. And most of these people, they don't care for anyone that's not white. They think that everyone that's not white is stupid."

I told him, "see I told you that in the beginning."

He told me, "I'm a man without a country. I don't know where to go or what to do."

* * *

I had about sixty days left, sixty-four, sixty-five days left of doing, in the Nam, down south and I was singing a song I made up from another tune, and it was Snobby

Going Back to Where the Rats and the Roaches Roam, and this guy next to me, said to me, "what do you mean, you got rats in your house?"

So I turned to him and he was a hunk, I turned to him and I said, "yeah, I got rats and roaches in my house, don't you have any in yours?" And he said to me, no, and he'd never seen a rat. And it started me thinking because soon I would be going back home and he would be going back home. I would be going back to the rats and the roaches, because I knew they were there. And if you come home right now you can hear them if you're eating in my kitchen; you'll hear them talking. And he would be going back to his nice California pad. And for me, the problem would begin again, and for him there would be no problem.

* * *

We were in this fox hole and the **CO**, he was one of the most scared people I've ever seen doing any kind of an operation, and we were being artilleried by the North Vietnamese artillery batteries in the **DMZ**, the mountain areas. And he was speaking to another lieutenant and he was saying, "the coons are getting out of hand." He looked over at the other corner of the bunker and he saw me, and he quickly changed his statement from " 'coo' . . . to *colored* people are getting out of hand." Now, right away it doesn't make me feel like I want to help him or I want to serve his cause. And from before I didn't have any kind of a feeling for it to start with.

CO was military slang for commanding officer.

The **DMZ**, or Demilitarized Zone, divided North and South Vietnam.

* * *

Well, I have one pretty sharp experience about this elderly Vietnamese woman. I was in charge of giving out the **C-rats** one day. And this elderly Vietnamese women came along with a crowd of children and she kept begging me for one of the C-rats. And I tell her "no, no, no, no, no." And I was laughing with her and the children. And this woman kept begging me for one whole hour, she kept begging me. And finally I looked at her and I saw in this woman's face, you know, real sincere, begging.

C-rats, or C-rations, were canned meals produced for the U.S. military.

And then I thought to myself, this woman could be my mother, or she could be my grandmother. And that child that she's holding in her hand could've been a relative of mine. And here she is begging for food. And I got so much on her side I started coming out of a pity bag. And I just reached down into the box and gave her two whole boxes of the C-rations. And they, you know, the other guys' food. And they were pretty riled up because I had taken their food and given it to her.

But I couldn't help it really because it was her land we'd come here to destroy and she needed food for the child. But the best part of it was, she went away and about two hours later when we were getting ready to leave she brought back a bag of roasted peanuts for me, and she gave it to me, and she wanted me to eat it right there to show her that I appreciated the bag of peanuts and I gave it to her. It just showed that really you want to help people and then the best thing to do is to give them food, clothes, instead of going over and trying to tell them what to do. And this really played a heavy part on me because it brought the Vietnamese people through this lady closer to me or closer to understanding them and their problems.

* * *

There was a survey made in the Marine Corps and they wanted to know what the marines felt about the Vietnamese people. How they felt about them. And it surprised many of the officers that most of the men came back saying that they thought the Vietnamese weren't human and because they don't think the Vietnamese are human then they treat them less than human. They think they're pigs, dogs, and everything else.

I'm pretty disgusted and I won't hide that. And I'm pretty angry. Angry about the whole mess. Not only black veterans but angry about the way black people have been treated on a whole and everyone knows what's going on and still yet, people, there's some people insist that nothing is going bad and things are going for the better, and we know that nothing is going for the better.

I have been made even more angry by going to Vietnam and having to contribute and seeing black youth die in Vietnam and still yet coming back and no one wants to listen to us; no one wants to hear what we have to say, and no one wants to do anything for us. We're still being treated as sub-humans. I've come back from Vietnam and I've seen the things in my neighborhood. I walk through the alleys and the alleys are piling high with garbage. I see young children, young black children running through the streets. They don't have the proper clothes on. And it's not the same old lie that their parents don't want to work. That is not the case. The case is they can't find jobs.

The Man was a slang reference to authority—particularly of the government.

Now, the people complain about welfare. They complain about what is being paid to these people now. Well, we didn't think up the welfare scheme. We didn't think up the welfare agency idea. **The Man** thought up the idea. He is the one that put it into practice. And he put it into practice to hide us. He paid enormous sums of money for two rooms that the welfare agencies would pay something like $150, and these weren't two good rooms. I can take you and show them to you right now. They were rat infested rooms. The plaster, holes in the wall, broken. The ceiling's corroding. And they paid this money to the people to keep them off the streets to hide them. And then they built subways and they built the subways under us so they would never have to see us.

But they did something wrong when they built those skyscrapers because then we could see the skyscrapers and we saw what they were putting out. And then we started crawling out of our neighborhoods and taking looks at what the Man had. And because we saw what the Man had, then we became more angry.

And it's now because these people are demanding that they get what's theirs. Now the Man says do away with welfare. He says these people are lazy. They're always collecting welfare. Well, Man, it was your idea. It wasn't our idea. So crawl off our backs.

These people didn't want to hide to start with. They asked you for jobs in the beginning. You didn't want to give them the jobs; you didn't want to give them the better education; you didn't want to give them the housing. Instead, you chose to give them charity.

And now you're complaining because you have to pay out more charity than you want to pay out. I mean don't complain to us, if you wanted to do free giving in the beginning. Continue to give free giving. Just because you started out giving a man a dollar and he's asking you for two dollars now, don't start crying on our shoulders. It's not our problem.

* * *

You know, I think one of the worst mistakes that the Man has ever made is to think that we would be fool enough to be trained in warfare and still yet come back home, watch our people live in misery, die in misery, and still be stupid enough not to want to help our people.

Now if the people on the street, the people in the so-called riots. I call them revolts. If the people in the revolts are to be shot down and killed, then I don't think there is any brother who is going to stand around knowing what he can do and knowing what he is capable of putting out, he's going to stand around and watch his own people get shot down. If a man on the street dies, I die. If this country ever decides to exterminate black people, I'm sure they are not going to exclude me because I've been in Vietnam. They're going to exterminate all black people and that includes all Vietnam veterans.

* * *

But they're not going to do it. If the United States government were ever to pull out of Vietnam and you asked them what happened to the 80 billion dollars they spent in Vietnam. Why can't they put it in our black communities? They're going to say they don't have the money. Well, where did all the money disappear to?

* * *

You know, this revolution is filled with so many ironies, really. First you tell us it's manly to keep your word. Right? If you are a man you keep you word and now all of the black people in this country are demanding—and even all of the black people in the world are demanding—is that you keep your word. You told us we were free. Well then, show us we are free. You told us there was justice, equality for all in this country. Well then stick to your word, and let us see the justice and equality for all, or else admit to us that you are not a man, you're a worm; you're afraid of us. You're afraid to give us equal stead. You're afraid that if you give us equal ground that we will match you and we will override you. And if that's what you're afraid of then tell us that's what you're afraid of but don't keep hiding it from us and holding this up to us and every time we ask you for something, you give us a little bit of something. It's all tokenism. We don't want tokenism.

And then most black men in this world don't want charity but yet every time we ask you for something you give us a little piece, a little piece. You're playing games with us. We're not children. We're big men. I've seen my father have to put up with all kinds of stuff. He was a big man. He raised a family. He went down south and he had to go around to the back door with his wife. We're not asking for anything. We're not asking for any favors. All we want is what's ours.

Now there are many black veterans who are coming back and they are mad, they're angry. Do you think they're going to sit down through this? Our fathers didn't have the knowledge that we have. They sat through it but there are other black youth that are not going to sit through it. We know about **Che**, we know about **Fanon**. We've read the books about our revolution. We've listened to **Mao** and his quotations. We know where we stand. We're not going to sit for it. We're asking, and if we ask and we don't get, we are prepared to stand up and take it.

Che Guevara was a charismatic Marxist revolutionary and major figure in the Cuban Revolution. He was killed in Bolivia in 1967.

Frantz Fanon was a Marxist critic of colonialism. His 1961 book *The Wretched of the Earth* argued that decolonization was, by necessity, a violent process.

Mao Zedong was the leader of the Chinese Communist Party and the author of the influential 1937 book *On Guerrilla Warfare*.

If I ask a man, I tell a man that I am hungry, I tell him I am cold, and I ask him to do something about my condition, and this man holds a loaf of bread right in front of me so I can see it, and I keep asking him, I'm begging him, to please give me a slice of the loaf of bread. I am hungry. Then it is known by every psychologist that the next step in the progression is that I am going to knock him upside the head and take the bread from him. I'm not going to starve to death.

All we're asking . . . No one wants to see blood, no one likes the smell of blood. No one wants war. Anyone who has been in war doesn't want war. Everyone knows what it is to see the inside of man's gut hanging out and see your friends die, see relatives die, no one wants to regress back to the state of mind where you have to think, it's all for the cause, therefore my mother has to die, my wife has to die, my brothers and sisters have to die, no one wants that. But you're pushing us to it. You're leaving us no choice. We are asking. We're begging. The students up at Columbia, they asked. The brothers down south asked. The brothers in Latin America, the brothers in Africa, they are all asking. All they're doing is asking.

Our fathers asked, our grandfathers asked. The presidents of our universities, our colleges, have to go to your back doors to beg that their children could be given just enough money so that they could be taught something to live off. And yet still they ask and ask and ask and you refused to give them anything. We're just about out of patience. We're not going to ask anymore.

The news media says that it's only the young that are militant, only the young that want this and want that. Okay, but we're 40% of the black population now. Or we were a year ago and still yet we're climbing. Before long we'll be 50%, 55%. Then we'll have the command.

We're not going to take it. We're not going to take sitting in rotten parks and places that just aren't fit for living. We're not going to take it. There's a limit to a man's patience and everyone knows that God, Christ, heaven . . . everyone knows that what we're asking is not a million dollars. All we're asking for is humanity. We're asking to be allowed to live like human beings and God, you tell us that this is too much to ask. You're sick. You're definitely sick. How can you tell me that it's too much to ask to be a human being?

LYNDON B. JOHNSON

Remarks upon Creating a Department of Transportation, October 15, 1966

The U.S. Department of Transportation was created as well as a cabinet-level secretary by merging parts of the Department of Commerce with the Federal Aviation Administration. In this speech, President Johnson outlines various projects associated with the construction, maintenance, and oversight of infrastructure projects throughout the nation.

SOURCE: *Lyndon B. Johnson, "Remarks upon Signing Bill Creating a Department of Transportation."* Weekly Compilation of Presidential Documents, *National Archives and Records Service, vol. 2, no. 42, 1966, pp. 1498–1500.*

We are deeply grateful for your presence in the East Room of the White House today.

In a large measure, America's history is a history of her transportation.

Our early cities were located by deep water harbors and inland waterways; they were nurtured by ocean vessels and by flatboats.

The railroad allowed us to move east and west. A thousand towns and more grew up along the railroad's gleaming rails.

The automobile stretched out over cities and created suburbia in America.

Trucks and modern highways brought bounty to remote regions.

Airplanes helped knit our Nation together, and knitted it together with other nations throughout the world.

And today, all Americans are really neighbors.

Transportation is the biggest industry we have in this country. It involves one out of every five dollars in our economy.

Our system of transportation is the greatest of any country in the world.

But we must face facts. We must be realistic. We must know—and we must have the courage to let our people know—that our system is no longer adequate.

During the next two decades, the demand for transportation in this country is going to more than double. But we are already falling far behind with the demand as it is. Our lifeline is tangled.

Lady Bird Johnson, the First Lady, was especially interested in highway beautification.

Today we are confronted by traffic jams. Today we are confronted by commuter crises, by crowded airports, by crowded airlanes, by screeching airplanes, by archaic equipment, by safety abuses, and roads that scar our Nation's beauty.

We have come to this historic East Room of the White House today to establish and to bring into being a Department of Transportation, the second Cabinet office to be added to the President's Cabinet in recent months.

This Department of Transportation that we are establishing will have a mammoth task—to untangle, to coordinate, and to build the national transportation system for America that America is deserving of.

And because the job is great, I intend to appoint a strong man to fill it. The new Secretary will be my principal adviser and my strong right arm on all transportation matters. I hope he will be the best equipped man in this country to give leadership to the country, to the President, to the Cabinet, to the Congress.

Among the many duties the new department will have, several deserve very special notice.

—To improve the safety in every means of transportation, safety of our automobiles, our trains, our planes, and our ships.

—To bring new technology to every mode of transportation by supporting and promoting research and development.

—To solve our most pressing transportation problems.

A day will come in America when people and freight will move through this land of ours speedily, efficiently, safely, dependably, and cheaply. That will be a good day and a great day in America.

Our transportation system was built by the genius of free enterprise. And as long as I am President, it will be sustained by free enterprise.

In a few respects, this bill falls short of our original hopes. It does not include the Maritime Administration. As experience is gained in the department, I would hope that the Congress could reexamine its decision to leave this key transportation activity alone, outside its jurisdiction.

But what is most important, I think, is that you, for the first time in modern history, have created and have brought for me to sign, a measure giving us a new Cabinet department. It was proposed, it will be established, and it will be in operation in the same year. All of these things took place in the same year.

It is the second major step in bringing our Government up to date with the times. Last year this Congress established the Department of Housing and Urban Affairs.

Today you bring 31 agencies and their bureaus, going in all directions, into a single Department of Transportation under the guidance and leadership of a Secretary of Transportation.

I think in fairness, candor requires me to review that this recommendation was made many years ago by the Hoover Commission, headed by the distinguished former President. This recommendation was urged upon the Congress and the people, and recommended many years ago by a most distinguished and popular President, President Dwight David Eisenhower.

This recommendation was made and urged upon the President and the Congress many years ago by the Senate Commerce Committee, and by dozens and dozens of enlightened, intelligent Members of both Houses of both parties.

What we are here today to do is to salute the Members of both parties, the leadership of both parties, and everyone who contributed to finally bringing our performance in line with our promise.

And I don't guess it would be good to say this, and I may even be criticized for saying it, but this, in effect, is another coonskin on the wall.

HUEY P. NEWTON AND BOBBY SEALE

Black Panther Ten Point Plan, 1966

The Black Panthers originally released this manifesto as a clarification of their position in 1966. Bobby Seale and Huey P. Newton regularly published it in the Black Panther newspaper. This version was published in 1969, but it is very close to the 1966 versions. Note how their ending parallels the Declaration of Independence.

SOURCE: The Black Panther, *vol. 3, no. 2, May 4, 1969, p. 16.*

1. We want freedom. We want power to determine the destiny of our Black Community.

We believe that black people will not be free until we are able to determine our destiny.

2. We want full employment for our people.

We believe that the federal government is responsible and obligated to give every man employment or a guaranteed income. We believe that if the white American businessmen will not give full employment, then the means of production should be taken from the businessmen and placed in the community so that the people of the community can organize and employ all of its people and give a high standard of living.

3. We want an end to the robbery by the white man of our Black Community.

We believe that this racist government has robbed us and now we are demanding the overdue debt of forty acres and two mules. Forty acres and two mules was promised 100 years ago as restitution for slave labor and mass murder of black people. We will accept the payment in currency which will be distributed to our many communities. The Germans are now aiding the Jews in Israel for the genocide of the Jewish people. The Germans murdered six million Jews. The American racist has taken part in the slaughter of over fifty million black people; therefore, we feel that this is a modest demand that we make.

4. We want decent housing, fit for shelter of human beings.

We believe that if the white landlords will not give decent housing to our black community, then the housing and the land should be made into cooperatives so that our community, with government aid, can build and make decent housing for its people.

5. We want education for our people that exposes the true nature of this decadent American society. We want education that teaches us our true history and our role in the present-day society.

We believe in an educational system that will give to our people a knowledge of self. If a man does not have knowledge of himself and his position in society and the world, then he has little chance to relate to anything else.

6. We want all black men to be exempt from military service.

We believe that Black people should not be forced to fight in the military service to defend a racist government that does not protect us. We will not fight and kill other people of color in the world who, like black people, are being victimized by the white racist government of America. We will protect ourselves from the force and violence of the racist police and the racist military, by whatever means necessary.

7. We want an immediate end to POLICE BRUTALITY and MURDER of black people.

We believe we can end police brutality in our black community by organizing black self-defense groups that are dedicated to defending our black community from racist police oppression and brutality. The Second Amendment to the Constitution of the United States gives a right to bear arms. We therefore believe that all black people should arm themselves for self-defense.

8. We want freedom for all black men held in federal, state, county and city prisons and jails.

We believe that all black people should be released from the many jails and prisons because they have not received a fair and impartial trial.

9. We want all black people when brought to trial to be tried in court by a jury of their peer group or people from their black communities, as defined by the Constitution of the United States.

We believe that the courts should follow the United States Constitution so that black people will receive fair trials. The 14th Amendment of the U.S. Constitution gives a man a right to be tried by his peer group. A peer is a person from a similar economic, social, religious, geographical, environmental, historical and racial background. To do this the court will be forced to select a jury from the black community from which the black defendant came. We have been, and are being tried by all-white juries that have no understanding of the "average reasoning man" of the black community.

10. We want land, bread, housing, education, clothing, justice and peace. And as our major political objective, a United Nations-supervised plebiscite to be held throughout the black colony in which only black colonial subjects will be allowed to participate, for the purpose of determining the will of black people as to their national destiny.

When, in the course of human events, it becomes necessary for one people to dissolve the political bands which have connected them with another, and to assume, among the powers of the earth, the separate and equal station to which the laws of nature and nature's God entitle them, a decent respect to the opinions of mankind requires that they should declare the causes which impel them to the separation.

We hold these truths to be self-evident, that all men are created equal, that they are endowed by their Creator with certain unalienable rights, that among these are life, liberty, and the pursuit of happiness. **That, to secure these rights, governments are instituted among men, deriving their just powers from the consent of the governed; that, whenever any form of government becomes destructive of these ends, it is the right of the people to alter or to abolish it, and to institute a new government, laying its foundation on such principles, and organizing its powers in such form, as to them shall seem most likely to effect their safety and happiness.** Prudence, indeed, will dictate that governments long established should not be changed for light and transient causes; and, accordingly, all experience hath shown, that mankind are more disposed to suffer, while evils are sufferable, than to right themselves by abolishing the forms to which they are accustomed. **But, when a long train of abuses and usurpations, pursuing invariably the same object, evinces a design to reduce them under absolute despotism, it is their right, it is their duty, to throw off such government, and to provide new guards for their future security.**

CASEY HAYDEN AND MARY KING

"Sex and Caste," 1966

Written in 1965 as a result of Hayden and King's work with the Student Nonviolent Coordinating Committee (SNCC), a multiracial civil rights organization composed of college students, this memorandum was initially circulated privately. The version here was published the following year in a radical, antiwar magazine. Although they were familiar with feminist authors like Simone de Beauvoir and Betty Friedan, Hayden and King used the more familiar language of the civil rights movement when framing their critique. Casey Hayden married SDS activist Tom Hayden in 1961. They divorced in 1965.

SOURCE: *Casey Hayden and Mary King, "Sex and Caste."* Liberation, *April 1966, pp. 35–36.*

We've talked a lot, to each other and to some of you, about our own and other women's problems in trying to live in our personal lives and in our work as independent and creative people. In these conversations we've found what seems to be recurrent ideas or themes. Maybe we can look at these things many of us perceive, often as a result of insights learned from the movement:

- Sex and caste: There seem to be many parallels that can be drawn between treatment of Negroes and treatment of women in our society as a whole. But in particular, women we've talked to who work in the movement seem to be caught up in a common-law caste system that operates, sometimes subtly, forcing them to work around or outside hierarchical structures of power which may exclude them. Women seem to be placed in the same position of assumed subordination in personal situations too. It is a caste system which, at its worst, uses and exploits women.

This is complicated by several facts, among them: 1) The caste system is not institutionalized by law (women have the right to vote, to sue for divorce, etc.); 2) Women can't withdraw from the situation (a la nationalism) or overthrow it; 3) There are biological differences (even though those biological differences are usually discussed or accepted without taking present and future technology into account so we probably can't be sure what these differences mean). Many people who are very hip to the implications of the racial caste system, even people in the movement, don't seem to be able to see the sexual caste system and if the question is raised they respond with: "That's the way it's supposed to be. There are biological differences." Or with other statements which recall a white segregationist confronted with integration.

- Women and problems of work: The caste system perspective dictates the roles assigned to women in the movement, and certainly even more to women outside the movement. Within the movement, questions arise in situations ranging from relationships of women organizers to men in the community, to who cleans the freedom house, to who holds leadership positions, to who does secretarial work, and who acts as spokesman for groups. Other problems arise between women with varying degrees of awareness of themselves as being as capable as men but held back from full participation, or between women who see themselves as needing more control of their work than other women demand. And there are problems with relationships between white women and black women.

- Women and personal relations with men: Having learned from the movement to think radically about the personal worth and abilities of people whose role in society had gone unchallenged before, a lot of women in the movement have begun trying to apply those lessons to their own relations with men. Each of us probably has her own story of the various results, and of the internal struggle occasioned by trying to break out of very deeply learned fears, needs, and self-perceptions, and of what happens when we try to replace them with concepts of people and freedom learned from the movement and organizing.

- Institutions: Nearly everyone has real questions about those institutions which shape perspectives on men and women: marriage, child-rearing patterns, women's (and men's) magazines, etc. People are beginning to think about and even to experiment with new forms in these areas.

- Men's reactions to the questions raised here: A very few men seem to feel, when they hear conversations involving these problems, that they have a right to be present and participate in them, since they are so deeply involved. At the same time, very few men can respond nondefensively, since the whole idea is either beyond their comprehension or threatens and exposes them. The usual response is laughter. That inability to see the whole issue as serious, as the strait-jacketing of both sexes, and as societally determined often shapes our own response so that we learn to think in their terms about ourselves and to feel silly rather than trust our inner feelings. The problems we're listing here, and what others have said about them, are therefore largely drawn from conversations among women only—and that difficulty in establishing dialogue with men is a recurring theme among people we've talked to.

- Lack of community for discussion: Nobody is writing, or organizing or talking publicly about women, in any way that reflects the problems that various women in the movement come across and which we've tried to touch above. Consider this quote from an article in the centennial issue of *The Nation*:

> However equally we consider men and women, the work plans for husbands and wives cannot be given equal weight. A woman should not aim for "a second-level career" because she is a *woman*; from girlhood on she should recognize that, if she is also going to be a wife and mother, she will not be able to give as much to her work as she would if single. That is, she should not feel that she cannot aspire to directing the laboratory simply because she is a woman, but rather because she is also a wife and mother; as such, her work as a lab technician (or the equivalent in another field) should bring both satisfaction and the knowledge that, through it, she is fulfilling an additional role, making an additional contribution.

And that's about as deep as the analysis goes publicly, which is not nearly so deep as we've heard many of you go in chance conversations.

The reason we want to try to open up dialogue is mostly subjective. Working in the movement often intensifies personal problems, especially if we start trying to apply things we're learning there to our personal lives. Perhaps we can start to talk with each other more openly than in the past and create a community of support for each other so we can deal with ourselves and others with integrity and can therefore keep working.

Objectively, the chances seem nil that we could start a movement based on anything as distant to general American thought as a sex-caste system. Therefore, most of us will probably want to work full time on problems such as war, poverty, race. The very fact that the country can't face, much less deal with, the questions we're raising means that the movement is one place to look for some relief. Real efforts at dialogue within the movement and with whatever liberal groups, community women, or students might listen are justified. That is, all the problems between men and women and all the problems of women functioning in society as equal human beings are among the most basic that people face. We've talked in the movement about trying to build a society which would see basic human problems (which are now seen as private troubles), as public problems and would try to shape institutions to meet human needs rather than shaping people to meet the needs of those with power. To raise questions like those above illustrates very directly that society hasn't dealt with some of its deepest problems and opens discussion of why that is so. (In one sense, it is a radicalizing question that can take people beyond legalistic solutions into areas of personal and institutional change.) The second objective reason we'd like to see discussion begin is that we've learned a great deal in the movement and perhaps this is one area where a determined attempt to apply ideas we've learned there can produce some new alternatives.

LYNDON B. JOHNSON

"Peace without Conquest," April 7, 1965

In this speech, which he gave at Johns Hopkins University, President Johnson outlines his justifications for escalating the war in Vietnam. By the end of 1968, over 16,000 American troops had been killed. In addition, over 87,000 had been seriously wounded.

SOURCE: *"Remarks by the President at Shriver Hall Auditorium, Johns Hopkins University, Baltimore, Md."* Congressional Record, *vol. 3, part 6, U.S. Government Printing Office, 1965, pp. 7493–7494.*

My fellow Americans, last week 17 nations sent their views to some dozen countries having interest in southeast Asia. We are joining these 17 countries in stating our American policy which we believe will contribute toward peace in this area.

Tonight I want to review once again with my own people the views of your Government.

Tonight Americans and Asians are dying for a world where each people may choose its own path to change.

This is the principle for which our ancestors fought in the valleys of Pennsylvania. It is the principle for which our sons fight in the jungles of Vietnam.

Vietnam is far from this quiet campus. We have no territory there, nor do we seek any. The war is dirty and brutal and difficult. And some 400 young men—born into an America bursting with opportunity and promise—have ended their lives on Vietnam's steaming soil.

Why must we take this painful road?

Why must this Nation hazard its ease, its interest, and its power for the sake of a people so far away?

We fight because we must fight if we are to live in a world where every country can shape its own destiny. And only in such a world will our own freedom be finally secure.

This kind of a world will never be built by bombs and bullets. Yet the infirmities of man are such that force must often precede reason—and the waste of war, the works of peace.

We wish this were not so. But we must deal with the world as it is, if it is ever to be as we wish.

THE NATURE OF THE CONFLICT

The world as it is in Asia is not a serene or peaceful place.

The first reality is that North Vietnam has attacked the independent nation of South Vietnam. Its object is total conquest.

Of course, some of the people of South Vietnam are participating in attack on their own Government. But trained men and supplies, orders, and arms, now in a constant stream from north to south.

This support is the heartbeat of the war.

And it is a war of unparalleled brutality. Simple farmers are the targets of assassination and kidnaping. Women and children are strangled in the night because their men are loyal to the government. Small and helpless villages are ravaged by sneak attacks. Large scale raids are conducted on towns, and terror strikes in the heart of cities.

The confused nature of this conflict cannot mask the fact that it is the new face of an old enemy. It is an attack by one country upon another. And the object of that attack is a friend to which we are pledged.

Over this war—and all Asia—is another reality: the deepening shadow of Communist China. The rulers in Hanoi are urged on by Peiping.[1] This is a regime which has destroyed freedom in Tibet, attacked India, and been condemned by the United Nations for aggression in Korea. It is a nation which is helping the forces of violence in almost every continent. The contest in Vietnam is part of a wider pattern of aggressive purpose.

WHY ARE WE IN VIETNAM

Why are these realities our concern? Why are we in South Vietnam?

We are there because we have a promise to keep. Since 1954 every American President has offered support to the people of South Vietnam. We have helped to build, and we have helped to defend. Thus, over many years, we have made a national pledge to help South Vietnam defend its independence.

I intend to keep our promise.

---

1. Beiping (or Peiping) was the name for the Chinese capital used by the Nationalist government of Taiwan, a U.S. ally.

To dishonor that pledge—to abandon this small and brave nation to its enemy—and to the terror that must follow—would be an unforgivable wrong.

We are also there to strengthen world order. Around the globe—from Berlin to Thailand—are people whose well-being rests, in part, on the belief they can count on us if they are attacked. To leave Vietnam to its fate would shake the confidence of all these people in the value of American commitment. The result would be increased unrest and instability, or even war.

We are also there because there are great stakes in the balance. Let no one think that retreat from Vietnam would bring an and to conflict. The battle would be renewed in one country and then another. The central lesson of our time is that the appetite of aggression is never satisfied. To withdraw from one battlefield, means only to prepare for the next. We must say in southeast Asia—as we did in Europe—in the words of the Bible: "Hitherto shalt thou come, but no further."

There are those who say that all our effort there will be futile—that China's power is such it is bound to dominate all southeast Asia. But there is no end to that argument until all the nations of Asia are swallowed up.

There are those who wonder why we have a responsibility there. We have it for the same reason we have a responsibility for the defense of freedom in Europe. World War II was fought in both Europe and Asia, and when it ended we found ourselves with continued responsibility for the defense of freedom.

OUR OBJECTIVE IN VIETNAM

Our objective is the independence of South Vietnam, and its freedom from attack. We want nothing for ourselves—only that the people of South Vietnam be allowed to guide their own country in their own way.

We will do everything necessary to reach that objective. And we will do only what is necessary.

In recent months, attacks on South Vietnam were stepped up. Thus, it became necessary to increase our response and make attacks by air. This is not a change of purpose. It is a change in what we believe that purpose requires.

We do this in order to slow down aggression.

We do this to increase the confidence of the brave people of South Vietnam who have bravely borne this brutal battle for so many years and with so many casualties.

And we do this to convince the leaders of North Vietnam—and all who seek to share their conquest—of a simple fact:

We will not be defeated.

We will not grow tired.

We will not withdraw, either openly or under the cloak of a meaningless agreement.

We know that air attacks alone will not accomplish all these purposes. But it is our best and prayerful Judgment that they are a necessary part of the surest road to peace.

We hope that peace will come swiftly. But that is in the hands of others beside ourselves. And we must be prepared for a long continued conflict. It will require patience as well as bravery—the will to endure as well as the will to resist.

I wish it were possible to convince others with words of what we now find it necessary to say with guns and planes: armed hostility is futile—our resources are equal to any challenge—because we fight for values and a principle, rather than territory or colonies, our patience and determination are unending.

Once this is clear, then it should also be clear that the only path for reasonable men is the path of peaceful settlement.

Such peace demands an independent South Vietnam—securely guaranteed and able to shape its own relationships to all others—free from outside interference—tied to no alliance—a military base for no other country.

These are essentials of any final settlement.

We will never be second in the search for such a peaceful settlement in Vietnam.

There may be many ways to this kind of peace: in discussion or negotiation with the governments concerned; in large groups or in small ones; in the reaffirmation of old agreements or their strengthening with new ones.

We have stated this position over and over again, 50 times—and more—to friend and foe alike. And we remain ready—with this purpose—for unconditional discussions.

And until that bright and necessary day of peace we will try to keep conflict from spreading. We have no desire to see thousands die in battle—Asians or Americans. We have no desire to devastate that which the people of North Vietnam have built with toll and sacrifice. We will use our power with restraint and with all the wisdom we can command.

But we will use it.

This war, like most wars, is filled with terrible irony. For what do the people of North Vietnam want? They want what their neighbors also desire: food for their hunger—health for their bodies and a chance to learn—progress for their country, and an end to the bondage of material misery. And they would find all these things far more readily in peaceful association with others than in the endless course of battle.

These countries of southeast Asia are homes for millions of impoverished people. Each day these people rise at dawn and struggle through weary hours to wrestle existence from the soil. They are often wracked by disease, plagued by hunger, and death comes early, at the age of 40.

Stability and peace do not come easily in such a land. Neither independence nor human dignity will be won by arms alone. It also requires the works of peace.

The American people have helped generously in these works.

Now there must be a much more massive effort to improve the life of man in the conflict-torn corner of the world.

A COOPERATIVE EFFORT FOR DEVELOPMENT

The first step is for the countries of southeast Asia to associate themselves in a greatly expanded cooperative effort for development. We would hope that North Vietnam will take its place in the common effort just as soon as peaceful cooperation is possible.

The United Nations is already actively engaged in development in this area. I would hope that the Secretary General of the United Nations could use the prestige of his great office—and his deep knowledge of Asia—to initiate, as soon as possible, with the countries of the area, a plan for cooperation in increased development.

For our part I will ask the Congress to join in a billion-dollar American investment in this effort when it is underway.

And I hope all other industrialized countries—including the Soviet Union—will join in this effort to replace despair with hope, and terror with progress.

The task is nothing less than to enrich the hopes and existence of more than a hundred million people. And there is much to be done.

The vast Mekong River can provide food and water and power on a scale to dwarf even our own TVA.

The wonders of modern medicine can be spread through villages where thousands die for lack of care.

Schools can be established to train people in the skills needed to manage the process of development.

And these objectives, and more, are within the reach of a cooperative and determined effort.

I also intend to expand and speed up a program to make available our farm surplus to assist in feeding and clothing the needy in Asia. We should not allow people to go hungry and naked while our own warehouses overflow with an abundance of wheat and corn, rice and cotton.

I will very shortly name a special team of patriotic and distinguished Americans to inaugurate our participation in these programs. This team will be headed by Mr. Eugene Black, the very able former president of the World Bank.

In areas still ripped by conflict, development will not be easy. Peace will be necessary for final success. But we cannot wait for peace to begin the job.

THE DREAM OF WORLD ORDER

This will be a disorderly planet for a long time. In Asia, as elsewhere, the forces of the modern world are shaking old ways and uprooting ancient civilizations. There will be turbulence and struggle and even violence. Great social change—as we see in our own country—does not always come without conflict.

We must also expect that nations will on occasion be in dispute with us. It may be because we are rich, or powerful—or because we have made mistakes—or because they honestly fear our intentions. However, no nation need ever fear that we desire their land, or to impose our will, or to dictate their institutions.

But we will always oppose the effort of one nation to conquer another.

We will do this because our own security is at stake.

But there is more to it than that. For our generation has a dream. It is a very old dream. But we have the power and the opportunity to make it real.

For centuries nations have struggled among each other. But we dream of a world where disputes are settled by law and reason. And we will try to make it so.

For most of history, men have hated and killed one another in battle. But we dream of an end to war. And we will try to make it so.

For all existence most men have lived in poverty, threatened by hunger. But we dream of a world where all are fed and charged with hope. And we will help to make it so.

POSSIBILITIES OF PEACE

The ordinary men and women of North Vietnam and South Vietnam—of China and India—or Russia and America—are brave people. They are filled with the same proportions of hate and fear, of love and hope. Most of them want the same things for themselves and their families. Most of them do not want their sons to die in battle, or see the homes of others destroyed.

This can be their world yet. Man now has the knowledge—always before denied—to make this planet serve the real needs of the people who live on it.

I know this will not be easy. I know how difficult it is for reason to guide passion, and love to master hate. The complexities of this world do not bow easily to pure and consistent answers.

But the simple truths are there just the same. We must all try to follow them as best we can.

We often say how impressive power is. But I do not find it impressive. The guns and bombs, the rockets and warships, are all symbols of human failure. They are necessary symbols. They protect what we cherish. But they are witness to human folly.

A dam built across a great river is impressive.

In the countryside where I was born. I have seen the night illuminated, the kitchens warmed and the homes heated, where once the cheerless night and the ceaseless cold held sway. And all this happened because electricity came to our town along the humming wires of the Rural Electrification Administration. Electrification of the countryside is impressive.

A rich harvest in a hungry land is impressive.

The sight of healthy children in a classroom is impressive.

These—not mighty arms—are the achievements which the American nation believes to be impressive.

And—if we are steadfast—the time may come when all other nations will also find it so.

We may well be living in the time foretold many years ago when it was said: "I call heaven and earth to record this day against you, that I have set before you life and death, blessing and cursing: therefore choose life, that both thou and thy seed may live."

This generation of the world must choose: destroy or build, kill or aid, hate or understand.

We can do all these things on a scale never dreamed of before.

We will choose life. And so doing we will prevail over the enemies within man, and over the natural enemies of all mankind.

STUDENTS FOR A DEMOCRATIC SOCIETY

Port Huron Statement, 1964

Initially drafted by SDS member Tom Hayden in 1962, the text of the group's manifesto was revised before being published in 1964. Written from the point of view of relatively affluent college students, it is far-ranging in its critique of American society. It attempts to imagine a better, less materialistic world.

SOURCE: *Students for a Democratic Society,* Port Huron Statement. *Students for a Democratic Society, 1964, pp. 3–11, 14–15.*

INTRODUCTION: AGENDA FOR A GENERATION

We are people of this generation, bred in at least modest comfort, housed now in universities, looking uncomfortably to the world we inherit.

When we were kids the United States was the wealthiest and strongest country in the world; the only one with the atom bomb, the least scarred by modern war, an initiator of the United Nations that we thought would distribute Western influence throughout the world. Freedom and equality for each individual, government of, by, and for the people—these American values we found good, principles by which we could live as men. Many of us began maturing in complacency.

As we grew, however, our comfort was penetrated by events too troubling to dismiss. First, the permeating and victimizing fact of human degradation, symbolized by the Southern struggle against racial bigotry, compelled most of us from silence to activism. Second, the enclosing fact of the Cold War, symbolized by the presence of the Bomb, brought awareness that we ourselves, and our friends, and millions of abstract "others" we knew more directly because of our common peril, might die at any time. We might deliberately ignore, or avoid, or fail to feel all other human problems, but not these two, for these were too immediate and crushing in their impact, too challenging in the demand that we as individuals take the responsibility for encounter and resolution.

While these and other problems either directly oppressed us or rankled our consciences and became our own subjective concerns, we began to see complicated and disturbing paradoxes in our surrounding America. The declaration "all men are created equal . . ." rang hollow before the facts of Negro life in the South and the big cities of the North. The proclaimed peaceful intentions of the United States contradicted its economic and military investments in the Cold War status quo.

We witnessed, and continue to witness, other paradoxes. With nuclear energy whole cities can easily be powered, yet the dominant nation-states seem more likely to unleash destruction greater than that incurred in all wars of human history. Although our own technology is destroying old and creating new forms of social organization, men still tolerate meaningless work and idleness. While two-thirds of mankind suffers undernourishment, our own upper classes revel amidst superfluous abundance. Although world population is expected to double in forty years, the nations still tolerate anarchy as a major principle of international conduct and uncontrolled exploitation governs the sapping of the earth's physical resources. Although mankind desperately needs revolutionary leadership, America rests in national stalemate, its goals ambiguous and tradition-bound instead of informed and clear, its democratic system apathetic and manipulated rather than "of, by, and for the people."

Not only did tarnish appear on our image of American virtue, not only did disillusion occur when the hypocrisy of American ideals was discovered, but we began to sense that what we had originally seen as the American Golden Age was actually the decline of an era. The worldwide outbreak of revolution against colonialism and imperialism, the entrenchment of totalitarian states, the menace of war, overpopulation, international disorder, supertechnology—these trends were testing the tenacity of our own commitment to democracy and freedom and our abilities to visualize their application to a world in upheaval.

Our work is guided by the sense that we may be the last generation in the experiment with living. But we are a minority—the vast majority of our people regard the temporary equilibriums of our society and world as eternally-functional parts. In this is perhaps the outstanding paradox: we ourselves are imbued with urgency, yet the message of our society is that there is no viable alternative to the present. Beneath the reassuring tones of the politicians, beneath the common opinion that America will "muddle through," beneath the stagnation of those who have closed their minds to the future, is the pervading feeling that there simply are no alternatives, that our times have witnessed the exhaustion not only of Utopias, but of any new departures as well. Feeling the press of complexity upon the emptiness of life, people are fearful of the thought that at any moment things might be thrust out of control. They fear change itself, since change might smash whatever invisible framework seems to hold back chaos for them now. For most Americans, all crusades are suspect, threatening. The fact that each individual sees apathy in his fellows perpetuates the common reluctance to organize for change. The dominant institutions are complex enough to blunt the minds of their potential critics, and entrenched enough to swiftly dissipate or entirely repel the energies of protest and reform, thus limiting human expectancies. Then, too, we are a materially improved society, and by our own improvements we seem to have weakened the case for further change.

Some would have us believe that Americans feel contentment amidst prosperity—but might it not be better be called a glaze above deeply-felt anxieties about their role in the new world? And if these anxieties produce a developed indifference to human affairs, do they not as well produce a yearning to believe there *is* an alternative to the present, that something *can* be done to change circumstances in the school, the workplaces, the bureaucracies, the government? It is to this latter yearning, at once the spark and engine of change, that we direct our present appeal. The search for truly democratic alternatives to the present, and a commitment to social experimentation with them, is a worthy and fulfilling human enterprise, one which moves us and, we hope, others today. On such a basis do we offer this document of our convictions and analysis: as an effort in understanding and changing the conditions of humanity in the late twentieth century, an effort rooted in the ancient, still unfulfilled conception of man attaining determining influence over his circumstances of life.

VALUES

Making values explicit—an initial task in establishing alternatives—is an activity that has been devalued and corrupted. The conventional moral terms of the age, the politician moralities—"free world," "people's democracies"—reflect realities poorly, if at all, and seem to function more as ruling myths than as descriptive principles. But neither has our experience in the universities brought us moral enlightenment. Our professors and administrators sacrifice controversy to public relations; their curriculums change more slowly than the living events of the world; their skills and silence are purchased by investors in the arms race; passion is called unscholastic. The questions we might want raised—what is really important? can we live in a different and better way? if we wanted to change society, how would we do it?—are not thought to be questions of a "fruitful, empirical nature," and thus are brushed aside.

* * *

In suggesting social goals and values, therefore, we are aware of entering a sphere of some disrepute. Perhaps matured by the past, we have no sure formulas, no closed theories—but that does not mean values are beyond discussion and

Consider Casey Hayden and Mary King's "Sex and Caste" (p. 126) as you consider the use of gender in this section.

tentative determination. A first task of any social movement is to convince people that the search for orienting theories and the creation of human values is complex but worthwhile. We are aware that to avoid platitudes we must analyze the concrete conditions of social order. But to direct such an analysis we must use the guideposts of basic principles. Our own social values involve conceptions of human beings, human relationships, and social systems.

We regard *men* as infinitely precious and possessed of unfulfilled capacities for reason, freedom, and love. In affirming these principles we are aware of countering perhaps the dominant conceptions of man in the twentieth century: that he is a thing to be manipulated, and that he is inherently incapable of directing his own affairs. We oppose the depersonalization that reduces human beings to the status of things—if anything, the brutalities of the twentieth century teach that means and ends are intimately related, that vague appeals to "posterity" cannot justify the mutilations of the present. We oppose, too, the doctrine of human incompetence because it rests essentially on the modern fact that men have been "competently" manipulated into incompetence—we see little reason why men cannot meet with increasing skill the complexities and responsibilities of their situation, if society is organized not for minority, but for majority, participation in decision-making.

Men have unrealized potential for self-cultivation, self-direction, self-understanding, and creativity. It is this potential that we regard as crucial and to which we appeal, not to the human potentiality for violence, unreason, and submission to authority. The goal of man and society should be human independence: a concern not with image of popularity but with finding a meaning in life that is personally authentic; a quality of mind not compulsively driven by a sense of powerlessness, nor one which unthinkingly adopts status values, nor one which represses all threats to its habits, but one which has full, spontaneous access to present and past experiences, one which easily unites the fragmented parts of personal history, one which openly faces problems which are troubling and unresolved; one with an intuitive awareness of possibilities, an active sense of curiosity, an ability and willingness to learn.

This kind of independence does not mean egotistic individualism—the object is not to have one's way so much as it is to have a way that is one's own. Nor do we deify man—we merely have faith in his potential.

Human relationships should involve fraternity and honesty. Human interdependence is contemporary fact; human brotherhood must be willed, however, as a condition of future survival and as the most appropriate form of social relations. Personal links between man and man are needed, especially to go beyond the partial and fragmentary bonds of function that bind men only as worker to worker, employer to employee, teacher to student, American to Russian.

Loneliness, estrangement, isolation describe the vast distance between man and man today. These dominant tendencies cannot be overcome by better personnel management, nor by improved gadgets, but only when a love of man overcomes the idolotrous worship of things by man. As the individualism we affirm is not egoism, the selflessness we affirm is not self-elimination. On the contrary we, believe in generosity of a kind that imprints one's unique individual qualities in the relation to other men, and to all human activity. Further, to dislike isolation is not to favor the abolition of privacy; the latter differs from isolation in that occurs or is abolished according to individual will.

We would replace power rooted in possession, privileged, or circumstance by power and uniqueness rooted in love, reflectiveness, reason, and creativity. As a *social system* we seek the establishment of a democracy of individual participation, governed by two central aims: that the individual share in those social decisions determining the quality and direction of his life; that society be organized to encourage independence in men and provide the media for their common participation.

In a participatory democracy, the political life would be based in several root principles:

> that decision-making of basic social consequence be carried on by public groupings;
>
> that politics be seen positively, as the art of collectively creating an acceptable pattern of social relations;
>
> that politics has the function of bringing people out of isolation and into community, thus being a necessary, though not sufficient, means of finding meaning in personal life;
>
> that the political order should serve to clarify problems in a way instrumental to their solution; it should provide outlets for the expression of personal grievance and aspiration; opposing views should be organized so as to illuminate choices and facilitate the attainment of goals; channels should be commonly available to relate men to knowledge and to power so that private problems—from bad recreation facilities to personal alienation—are formulated as general issues.

The economic sphere would have as its basis the principles:

> that work should involve incentives worthier than money or survival. It should be educative, not stultifying; creative, not mechanical; self-directed, not manipulated, encouraging independence, a respect for others, a sense of dignity and a willingness to accept social responsibility, since it is this experience that has crucial influence on habits, perceptions and individual ethics;
>
> that the economic experience is so personally decisive that the individual must share in its full determination;
>
> that the economy itself is of such social importance that its major resources and means of production should be open to democratic participation and subject to democratic social regulation.

Students for a Democratic Society, Port Huron Statement, 1964

Like the political and economic ones, major social institutions—cultural, educational, rehabilitative, and others—should be generally organized with the well-being and dignity of man as the essential measure of success.

In social change or interchange, we find violence to be abhorrent because it requires generally the transformation of the target, be it a human being or a community of people, into a depersonalized object of hate. It is imperative that the means of violence be abolished and the institutions—local, national, international—that encourage non-violence as a condition of conflict be developed.

These are our central values, in skeletal form. It remains vital to understand their denial or attainment in the context of the modern world.

THE STUDENTS

In the last few years, thousands of American students demonstrated that they at least felt the urgency of the times. They moved actively and directly against racial injustices, the threat of war, violations of individual rights of conscience and, less frequently, against economic manipulation. They succeeded in restoring a small measure of controversy to the campuses after the stillness of the **McCarthy period**. They succeeded, too, in gaining some concessions from the people and institutions they opposed, especially in the fight against racial bigotry.

The **McCarthy period** broadly refers to virulent anticommunist investigations epitomized by hearings staged by Senator Joseph McCarthy in the early 1950s, during the Cold War.

The significance of these scattered movements lies not in their success or failure in gaining objectives—at least not yet. Nor does the significance lie in the intellectual "competence" or "maturity" of the students involved—as some pedantic elders allege. The significance is in the fact the students are breaking the crust of apathy and overcoming the inner alienation that remain the defining characteristics of American college life.

If student movements for change are still rareties on the campus scene, what is commonplace there? The real campus, the familiar campus, is a place of private people, engaged in their notorious "inner emigration." It is a place of commitment to business-as-usual, getting ahead, playing it cool. It is a place of mass affirmation of the Twist, but mass reluctance toward the controversial public stance. Rules are accepted as "inevitable," bureaucracy as "just circumstances," irrelevance as "scholarship," selflessness as "martyrdom," politics as "just another way to make people, and an unprofitable one, too."

Almost no students value activity as citizens. Passive in public, they are hardly more idealistic in arranging their private lives: **Gallup** concludes they will settle for "low success, and won't risk high failure." There is not much willingness to take risks (not even in business), no settling of dangerous goals, no real conception of personal identity except one manufactured in the image of others, no real urge for personal fulfillment except to be almost as successful as the very successful people. Attention is being paid to social status (the quality of shirt collars, meeting people, getting wives or husbands,

Gallup polls had become trusted measures of public sentiment.

making solid contacts for later on); much, too, is paid to academic status (grades, honors, the med school rat race). But neglected generally is real intellectual status, the personal cultivation of the mind.

"Student don't even give a damn about the apathy," one has said. Apathy toward apathy begets a privately-constructed universe, a place of systematic study schedules, two nights each week for beer, a girl or two, and early marriage; a framework infused with personality, warmth, and under control, no matter how unsatisfying otherwise.

Under these conditions university life loses all revelvance to some. Four hundred thousand of our classmates leave college every year.

But apathy is not simply an attitude; it is a product of social institutions, and of the structure and organization of higher education itself. The extracurricular life is ordered according to *in loco parentis* theory, which ratifies the Administration as the moral guardian of the young.

The accompanying "let's pretend" theory of student extracurricular affairs validates student government as a training center for those who want to spend their lives in political pretense, and discourages initiative from the more articulate, honest, and sensitive students. The bounds and style of controversy are delimited before controvery begins. The university "prepares" the student for "citizenship" through perpetual rehearsals and, usually, through emasculation of what creative spirit there is in the individual.

The academic life contains reinforcing counterparts to the way in which extracurricular life is organized. The academic world is founded on a teacher-student relation analogous to the parent-child relation which characterizes *in loco parentis*. Further, academia includes a radical separation of the student from the material of study. That which is studied, the social reality, is "objectified" to sterility, dividing the student from life—just as he is restrained in active involvement by the deans controlling student government. The specialization of function and knowledge, admittedly necessary to our complex technological and social structure, has produced an exaggerated compartmentalization of study and understanding. This has contributed to an overly parochial view, by faculty, of the role of its research and scholarship, to a discontinuous and truncated understanding, by students, of the surrounding social order; and to a loss of personal attachment, by nearly all, to the worth of study as a humanistic enterprise.

There is, finally, the cumbersome academic bureaucracy extending throughout the academic as well as the extracurricular structures, contributing to the sense of outer complexity and inner powerlessness that transforms the honest searching of many students to a ratification of convention and, worse, to a numbness to present and future catastrophes. The size and financing systems of the university enhance the permanent trusteeship of the administrative bureaucracy, their power leading to a shift within the university toward the value standards of business and the administrative mentality. Huge foundations and other private financial interests shape the under-financed colleges and universities, not only making them more commercial, but less disposed to diagnose society critically, less open to dissent. Many social and physical scientists, neglecting the liberating heritage of higher learning, develop "human relations" or "morale-producing" techniques for the corporate economy, while others exercise their intellectual skills to accelerate the arms race.

Tragically, the university could serve as a significant source of social criticism and an initiator of new modes and molders of attitudes. But the actual intellectual effect of the college experience is hardly distinguishable from that of any other communications channel—say, a television set—passing on the stock truths of the day. Students leave college somewhat more "tolerant" than when they arrived, but basically unchallenged in their values and political orientations. With administrators ordering the institution, and faculty the curriculum, the student learns by his isolation to accept elite rule within the university, which prepares him to accept later forms of minority control. The real function of the educational system—as opposed to its more rhetorical function of "searching for truth"—is to impart the key information and styles that will help the student get by, modestly but comfortably, in the big society beyond.

THE SOCIETY BEYOND

Look beyond the campus, to America itself. That student life is more intellectual, and perhaps more comfortable, does not obscure the fact that the fundamental qualities of life on the campus reflect the habits of society at large. The fraternity president is seen at the junior manager levels; the sorority queen has gone to Grosse Pointe; the serious poet burns for a place, any place, to work; the once-serious and never-serious poets work at the advertising agencies. The desperation of people threatened by forces about which they know little and of which they can say less; the cheerful emptiness of people "giving up" all hope of changing things; the faceless ones polled by Gallup who listed "international affairs" fourteenth on their list of "problems" but who also expected thermonuclear war in the next few years; in these and other forms, Americans are in withdrawal from public life, from any collective effort at directing their own affairs.

Some regard these national doldrums as a sign of healthy approval of the established order—but is it approval by consent or manipulated acquiescence? Others declare that the people are withdrawn because compelling issues are fast disappearing—perhaps there are fewer breadlines in America, but is Jim Crow gone, is there enough work and work more fulfilling, is world war a diminishing threat, and what of the revolutionary new peoples? Still others think the national quietude is a necessary consequence of the need for elites to resolve complex and specialized problems of modern industrial society—but, then, why should *business* elites help decide foreign policy, and who controls the elites anyway, and are they solving mankind's problems? Others, finally, shrug knowingly and announce that full democracy never worked anywhere in the past—but why lump qualitatively different civilizations together, and how can a social order work well if its best thinkers are skeptics, and is man really doomed forever to the domination of today?

There are no convincing apologies for the contemporary malaise. While the world tumbles toward the final war, while men in other nations are trying desperately to alter events, while the very future qua future is uncertain—America is without community, impulse, without the inner momentum necessary for an age when societies cannot successfully perpetuate themselves by their military weapons, when democracy must be viable because of the quality of life, not its quantity of rockets.

The apathy here is, first *subjective*—the felt powerlessness of ordinary people, the resignation before the enormity of events. But subjective apathy is encouraged by the *objective* American situation—the actual structural separation of people from power, from relevant knowledge, from pinnacles of decision-making. Just as the university influences the student way of life, so do major social institutions create the circumstances in which the isolated citizen will try hopelessly to understand his world and himself.

The very isolation of the individual—from power and community and ability to aspire—means the rise of a democracy without publics. With the great mass of people structurally remote and psychologically hesitant with respect to democratic institutions, those institutions themselves attenuate and become, in the fashion of the vicious circle, progressively less accessible to those few who aspire to serious participation in social affairs. The vital democratic connection between community and leadership, between the mass and the several elites, has been so wrenched and perverted that disastrous policies go unchallenged time and again.

* * *

THE ECONOMY

American capitalism today advertises itself as the Welfare State. Many of us comfortably expect pensions, medical care, unemployment compensation, and other social services in our lifetimes. Even with one-fourth of our productive capacity unused, the majority of Americans are living in relative comfort—although their nagging incentive to "keep up" makes them continually dissatisfied with their possessions. In many places, unrestrained bosses, uncontrolled machines, and sweatshop conditions have been reformed or abolished and suffering tremendously relieved. But in spite of the benign yet obscuring effects of the New Deal reforms and the reassuring phrases of government economists and politicians, the paradoxes and myths of the economy are sufficient to irritate our complacency and reveal to us some essential causes of the American malaise.

We live amidst a national celebration of economic prosperity while poverty and deprivation remain an unbreakable way of life for millions in the "affluent society," including many of our own generation. We hear glib references to the "welfare state," "free enterprise," and "share-holder's democracy" while military defense is the main item of "public" spending and obvious oligopoly and other forms of minority rule defy real individual initiative or popular control. Work, too, is often unfulfilling and victimizing, accepted as a channel to status or plenty, if not a way to pay the bills, rarely as a means of understanding and controlling self and events. In work and leisure the individual is regulated as part of the system, a consuming unit, bombarded by hard-sell, soft-sell, lies and semi-true appeals to his basest drives. He is always told that he is a "free" man because of "free enterprise."

GEORGE WALLACE

"Inaugural Address," January 14, 1963

When Wallace delivered this speech from the steps of the state capitol building in Montgomery, Alabama, he stood in the same spot occupied by Jefferson Davis when he was sworn in as the president of the Confederacy. Written by Asa Carter, a member of both Wallace's staff and the Ku Klux Klan who later became a novelist, the speech gained Wallace national recognition as a defender of legal segregation in the South. He expressed a determination to stand against the "tyranny" of federal attempts to push the Deep South toward integration, and framed his resistance in terms of states' rights. When he launched his third-party candidacy for the presidency in 1968, Wallace built upon these foundations.

The speech begins with Wallace thanking a variety of people who helped him to get elected. Contrast this folksy charm with the blisteringly racist message that follows.

SOURCE: *"Inaugural Address of Governor George Wallace, January 14, 1963." Alabama Department of Archives and History.*

overnor Patterson, Governor Barnett, from one of the greatest states in this nation, Mississippi, Mayor Brown, representing Governor Hollings of South Carolina, Judge Perez—members of the Alabama Congressional Delegation, members of the Alabama Legislature, distinguished guests, fellow Alabamians:

Before I begin my talk with you, I want to ask you for a few minutes patience while I say something that is on my heart: I want to thank those home folks of my county who first gave an anxious country boy his opportunity to serve in State politics. I shall always owe a lot to those who gave me that first opportunity to serve.

I will never forget the warm support and close loyalty of the folks at Suttons, Haigler's Mill, Eufaula, Beat 6 and Beat 14,[1] Richards Cross Roads and Gammage Beat—at Baker Hill, Beat 8, and Comer, Spring Hill, Adams Chapel and Mount Andrew—White Oak, Baxter's Station, Clayton, Louisville and Cunningham Place; Horns Crossroads, Texasville and Blue Springs, where the vote was 304 for Wallace and 1 for the opposition—and the dear little lady whom I heard had made that one vote against me—by mistake—because she couldn't see too well—and she had pulled the wrong lever—Bless her heart. At Clio, my birthplace, and Elamville. I shall never forget them. May God bless them.

And I shall forever remember that election day morning as I waited—and suddenly at ten o'clock that morning the first return of a box was flashed over this state: it carried the message—Wallace 15, opposition zero; and it came from the Hamrick Beat at Putman's Mountain where live the great hill people of our state. May God bless the mountain man—his loyalty is unshakable, he'll do to walk down the road with.

I hope you'll forgive me these few moments of remembering—but I wanted them—and you—to know, that I shall never forget.

And I wish I could shake hands and thank all of you in this State who voted for me—and those of you who did not—for I know you voted your honest convictions—and now, we must stand together and move the great State of Alabama forward.

I would be remiss, this day, if I did not thank my wonderful wife and fine family for their patience, support and loyalty—and there is no man living who does not owe more to his mother than he can ever repay, and I want my mother to know that I realize my debt to her.

This is the day of my Inauguration as Governor of the State of Alabama. And on this day I feel a deep obligation to renew my pledges, my covenants with you—the people of this great state.

General Robert E. Lee[2] said that "duty" is the most sublime word in the English language and I have come, increasingly, to realize what he meant. I SHALL do my duty to you, God helping—to every man, to every woman—yes, and to every child in this State. I shall fulfill my duty toward honesty and economy in our State government so that no man shall have a part of his livelihood cheated and no child shall have a bit of his future stolen away.

---

1. Beats were voting districts in Alabama.
2. Robert E. Lee was the commanding general of the armies of the Confederacy.

I have said to you that I would eliminate the liquor agents in this state and that the money saved would be returned to our citizens—I am happy to report to you that I am now filling orders for several hundred one-way tickets and stamped on them are these words—"for liquor agents—destination:—out of Alabama." I am happy to report to you that the big-wheeling cocktail-party boys have gotten the word that their free whiskey and boat rides are over—that the farmer in the field, the worker in the factory, the businessman in his office, the housewife in her home, have decided that the money can be better spent to help our children's education and our older citizens—and they have put a man in office to see that it is done. It shall be done. Let me say one more time—no more liquor drinking in your governor's mansion.

I shall fulfill my duty in working hard to bring industry into our state, not only by maintaining an honest, sober and free-enterprise climate of government in which industry can have confidence—but in going out and getting it—so that our people can have industrial jobs in Alabama and provide a better life for their children.

I shall not forget my duty to our senior citizens—so that their lives can be lived in dignity and enrichment of the golden years, nor to our sick, both mental and physical—and they will know we have not forsaken them. I want the farmer to feel confident that in this State government he has a partner who will work with him in raising his income and increasing his markets. and I want the laboring man to know he has a friend who is sincerely striving to better his field of endeavor.

I want to assure every child that this State government is not afraid to invest in their future through education, so that they will not be handicapped on the very threshold of their lives.

Today I have stood, where once Jefferson Davis[3] stood, and took an oath to my people. It is very appropriate then that from this Cradle of the Confederacy, this very Heart of the Great Anglo-Saxon Southland, that today we sound the drum for freedom as have our generations of forebears before us done, time and again down through history. Let us rise to the call of freedom-loving blood that is in us and send our answer to the tyranny that clanks its chains upon the South. In the name of the greatest people that have ever trod this earth, I draw the line in the dust and toss the gauntlet before the feet of tyranny—and I say—segregation now—segregation tomorrow—segregation forever.

The Washington, D. C. school riot report is disgusting and revealing. We will not sacrifice our children to any such type school system—and you can write that down. The federal troops in Mississippi could better be used guarding the safety of the citizens of Washington, D. C., where it is even unsafe to walk or go to a ball game—and that is the nation's capitol [*sic*]. I was safer in a B-29 bomber over Japan during the war in an air raid, than the people of Washington are walking in the White House neighborhood. A closer example is Atlanta. The city officials fawn

3. Jefferson Davis was the president of the Confederate States of America.

for political reasons over school integration and THEN build barricades to stop residential integration—what hypocrisy!

Let us send this message back to Washington by our representatives who are with us today—that from this day we are standing up, and the heel of tyranny does not fit the neck of an upright man—that we intend to take the offensive and carry our fight for freedom across this nation, wielding the balance of power we know we possess in the Southland—that WE, not the insipid bloc voters of some sections—will determine in the next election who shall sit in the White House of these United States—that from this day—from this hour—from this minute—we give the word of a race of honor that we will tolerate their boot in our face no longer—and let those certain judges put that in their opium pipes of power and smoke it for what it is worth.

Hear me, Southerners! You sons and daughters who have moved north and west throughout this nation—we call on you from your native soil to join with us in national support and vote—and we know—wherever you are—away from the hearths of the Southland—that you will respond, for though you may live in the fartherest reaches of this vast country—your heart has never left Dixieland.

And you native sons and daughters of old New England's rock-ribbed patriotism—and you sturdy natives of the great Mid-West—and you descendants of the far West flaming spirit of pioneer freedom—we invite you to come and be with us—for you are of the Southern mind—and the Southern spirit—and the Southern philosophy—you are Southerners too and brothers with us in our fight.

What I have said about segregation goes double this day—and what I have said to or about some federal judges goes TRIPLE this day.

Alabama has been blessed by God as few states in this Union have been blessed. Our state owns ten per cent of all the natural resources of all the states in our country. Our inland waterway system is second to none—and has the potential of being the greatest waterway transport system in the entire world. We possess over thirty minerals in usable quantities and our soil is rich and varied, suited to a wide variety of plants. Our native pine and forestry system produces timber faster than we can cut it and yet we have only pricked the surface of the great lumber and pulp potential.

With ample rainfall and rich grasslands our livestock industry is in the infancy of a giant future that can make us a center of the big and growing meat packing and prepared foods marketing. We have the favorable climate, streams, woodlands, beaches, and natural beauty to make us a recreational mecca in the booming tourist and vacation industry. Nestled in the great Tennessee Valley, we possess the Rocket center of the world and the keys to the space frontier.[4]

While the trade with a developing Europe built the great port cities of the east coast, our own fast developing port of Mobile faces as a magnetic gateway to

4. The Marshall Space Flight Center in Huntsville, Alabama, is an important NASA facility.

After an innocuous and typical lead-in, Wallace shifts to a far-ranging critique of federal power.

the great continent of South America, well over twice as large and hundreds of times richer in resources, even now awakening to the growing probes of enterprising capital with a potential of growth and wealth beyond any present dream for our port development and corresponding results throughout the connecting waterways that thread our state.

And while the manufacturing industries of free enterprise have been coming to our state in increasing numbers, attracted by our bountiful natural resources, our growing numbers of skilled workers and our favorable conditions, their present rate of settlement here can be increased from the trickle they now represent to a stream of enterprise and endeavor, capital and expansion that can join us in our work of development and enrichment of the educational futures of our children, the opportunities of our citizens and the fulfillment of our talents as God has given them to us. To realize our ambitions and to bring to fruition our dreams, we as Alabamians must take cognizance of the world about us. We must re-define our heritage, re-school our thoughts in the lessons our forefathers knew so well, first hand, in order to function and to grow and to prosper. We can no longer hide our head in the sand and tell ourselves that the ideology of our free fathers is not being attacked and is not being threatened by another idea—for it is. We are faced with an idea that if a centralized government assumes enough authority, enough power over its people, that it can provide a utopian life—that if given the power to dictate, to forbid, to require, to demand, to distribute, to edict and to judge what is best and enforce that will of judgement upon its citizen from unimpeachable authority—then it will produce only "good"—and it shall be our father—and our God. It is an idea of government that encourages our fears and destroys our faith—for where there is faith, there is no fear, and where there is fear, there is no faith. In encouraging our fears of economic insecurity it demands we place that economic management and control with government; in encouraging our fear of educational development it demands we place that education and the minds of our children under management and control of government, and even in feeding our fears of physical infirmities and declining years, it offers and demands to father us through it all and even into the grave. It is a government that claims to us that it is bountiful as it buys its power from us with the fruits of its rapaciousness of the wealth that free men before it have produced and builds on crumbling credit without responsibilities to the debtors—our children. It is an ideology of government erected on the encouragement of fear and fails to recognize the basic law of our fathers that governments do not produce wealth—people produce wealth—free people; and as those people become less free—as they learn there is little reward for ambition—that it requires faith to risk—and they have none—as the government must restrict and penalize and tax incentive and endeavor and must increase its expenditures of bounties—then this government must assume more and more police powers and we find we are become government-fearing people—not God-fearing people. We find we have replaced faith with fear—and though we may give lip service to the

Almighty—in reality, government has become our god. It is, therefore, a basically ungodly government and its appeal to the psuedo-intellectual and the politician is to change their status from servant of the people to master of the people—to play at being God—without faith in God—and without the wisdom of God. It is a system that is the very opposite of Christ for it feeds and encourages everything degenerate and base in our people as it assumes the responsibilities that we ourselves should assume. Its psuedo-liberal spokesmen and some Harvard advocates have never examined the logic of its substitution of what it calls "human rights" for individual rights, for its propaganda play upon words has appeal for the unthinking. Its logic is totally material and irresponsible as it runs the full gamut of human desires—including the theory that everyone has voting rights without the spiritual responsibility of preserving freedom. Our founding fathers recognized those rights—but only within the frameworks of those spiritual responsibilities. But the strong, simple faith and sane reasoning of our founding fathers has long since been forgotten as the so-called "progressives" tell us that our Constitution was written for "horse and buggy" days—so were the Ten Commandments.

Not so long ago men stood in marvel and awe at the cities, the buildings, the schools, the autobahns that the government of Hitler's Germany had built—just as centuries before they stood in wonder at Rome's building—but it could not stand—for the system that built it had rotted the souls of the builders—and in turn—rotted the foundation of what God meant that men should be. Today that same system on an international scale is sweeping the world. It is the "changing world" of which we are told—it is called "new" and "liberal." It is as old as the oldest dictator. It is degenerate and decadent. As the national racism of Hitler's Germany persecuted a national minority to the whim of a national majority—so the international racism of the liberals seek to persecute the international white minority to the whim of the international colored majority—so that we are footballed about according to the favor of the Afro-Asian bloc. But the Belgian survivors of the Congo cannot present their case to a war crimes commission—nor the Portuguese of Angola—nor the survivors of Castro—nor the citizens of Oxford, Mississippi.

Wallace now shifts decisively into a racist argument regarding what he perceives as an international anti-white conspiracy.

It is this theory of international power politic that led a group of men on the Supreme Court for the first time in American history to issue an edict, based not on legal precedent, but upon a volume, the editor of which has said our Constitution is outdated and must be changed and the writers of which, some had admittedly belonged to as many as half a hundred communist-front organizations. It is this theory that led this same group of men to briefly bare the ungodly core of that philosophy in forbidding little school children to say a prayer.[5] And we find the evidence of that ungodliness even in the removal of the words "in God we trust" from some of our dollars, which was placed there as like evidence by our

5. *Engel v. Vitale* was a 1962 Supreme Court decision that ruled official school prayer unconstitutional.

founding fathers as the faith upon which this system of government was built. It is the spirit of power thirst that caused a president in Washington to take up Caesar's pen and with one stroke of it, make a law. A Law which the law making body of Congress refused to pass—a law that tells us that we can or cannot buy or sell our very homes, except by his conditions—and except at HIS discretion. It is the spirit of power thirst that led that same President to launch a full offensive of twenty-five thousand troops against a university—of all places—in his own country—and against his own people, when this nation maintains only six thousand troops in the beleagured city of Berlin.[6] We have witnessed such acts of "might makes right" over the world as men yielded to the temptation to play God—but we have never before witnessed it in America. We reject such acts as free men. We do not defy, for there is nothing to defy—since as free men we do not recognize any government right to give freedom—or deny freedom. No government erected by man has that right. As Thomas Jefferson has said, "The God who gave us life, gave us liberty at the same time; no king holds the right of liberty in his hands." Nor does any ruler in American government.

We intend, quite simply, to practice the free heritage as bequeathed to us as sons of free fathers. We intend to re-vitalize the truly new and progressive form of government that is less than two hundred years old—a government first founded in this nation simply and purely on faith—that there is a personal God who rewards good and punishes evil—that hard work will receive its just desserts—that ambition and ingenuity and incentiveness—and profit of such—are admirable traits and goals—that the individual is encouraged in his spiritual growth and from that growth arrives at a character that enhances his charity toward others and from that character and that charity so is influenced business, and labor and farmer and government. We intend to renew our faith as God-fearing men—<u>not</u> government-fearing men nor any other kind of fearing-men. We intend to roll up our sleeves and pitch in to develop this full bounty God has given us—to live full and useful lives and in absolute freedom from all fear. Then can we enjoy the full richness of the Great American Dream.

We have placed this sign, "In God We Trust," upon our State Capitol on this Inauguration Day as physical evidence of determination to renew the faith of our fathers and to practice the free heritage they bequeathed to us. We do this with the clear and solemn knowledge that such physical evidence is evidently a direct violation of the logic of that Supreme Court in Washington, D. C., and if they or their spokesmen in this state wish to term this defiance—I say—then let them make the most of it.

This nation was never meant to be a unit of one—but a united of the many—that is the exact reason our freedom-loving forefathers established the states, so as

6. This is a reference to the Kennedy administration's decision to use federalized National Guard troops to integrate the University of Alabama in 1963.

to divide the rights and powers among the many states, insuring that no central power could gain master government control.

In united effort we were meant to live under this government—whether Baptist, Methodist, Presbyterian, Church of Christ, or whatever one's denomination or religious belief—each respecting the others right to a separate denomination—each, by working to develop his own, enriching the total of all our lives through united effort. And so it was meant in our political lives—whether Republican, Democrat, Prohibition, or whatever political party—each striving from his separate political station—respecting the rights of others to be separate and work from within their political framework—and each separate political station making its contribution to our lives—

Wallace now shifts more overtly to his reasons for supporting segregation.

And so it was meant in our racial lives—each race, within its own framework has the freedom to teach—to instruct—to develop—to ask for and receive deserved help from others of separate racial stations. This is the great freedom of our American founding fathers—but if we amalgamate into the one unit as advocated by the communist philosophers—then the enrichment of our lives—the freedom for our development—is gone forever. We become, therefore, a mongrel unit of one under a single all powerful government—and we stand for everything—and for nothing.

The true brotherhood of America, of respecting the separateness of others—and uniting in effort—has been so twisted and distorted from its original concept that there is small wonder that communism is winning the world.

We invite the negro citizens of Alabama to work with us from his separate racial station—as we will work with him—to develop, to grow in individual freedom and enrichment. We want jobs and a good future for BOTH our races. We want to help the physically and mentally sick of BOTH races—the tubercular and the infirm. This is the basic heritage of my religion, of which I make full practice—for we are all the handiwork of God.

But we warm those, of any group, who would follow the false doctrine of communistic amalgamation that we will not surrender our system of government—our freedom of race and religion for that freedom was won at a hard price, and if it requires a hard price to keep it—we are able—and quite willing to pay it.

The liberals' theory that poverty, discrimination and lack of opportunity is the cause of communism is a false theory—if it were true the South would have been the biggest single communist bloc in the western hemisphere long ago—for after the great War Between the States, our people faced a desolate land of burned universities, destroyed crops and homes, with manpower depleted and crippled, and even the mule, which was required to work the land, was so scarce that whole communities shared one animal to make the spring plowing. There were no government hand-outs, no Marshall Plan aid, no coddling to make sure that our people would not suffer; instead the South was set upon by the vulturous

Wallace draws upon a familiar racist conception of the history of the Reconstruction era that followed the American Civil War.

carpetbagger and federal troops, all loyal Southerners were denied the vote at the point of bayonet, so that the infamous, illegal 14th Amendment might be passed. There was no money, no food and no hope of either. But our grandfathers bent their knee only in church and bowed their head only to God.

Not for one single instant did they ever consider the easy way of federal dictatorship and amalgamation in return for fat bellies. They fought. They dug sweet roots from the ground with their bare hands and boiled them in the old iron pots—they gathered poke salad from the woods and acorns from the ground. They fought. They followed no false doctrine—they knew what they wanted—and they fought for freedom! They came up from their knees in the greatest display of sheer nerve, grit and guts that has ever been set down in the pages of written history—and they won! The great writer, Rudyard Kipling, wrote of them, that: "There in the Southland of the United States of America, lives the greatest fighting breed of man—in all the world!"

And that is why today, I stand ashamed of the fat, well-fed whiners who say that it is inevitable—that our cause is lost. I am ashamed of them—and I am ashamed for them. They do not represent the people of the Southland.

And may we take note of one other fact, with all the trouble with communists that some sections of this country have—there are not enough native communists in the South to fill up a telephone booth—and THAT is a matter of public FBI record.

We remind all within hearing of this Southland that a Southerner, Peyton Randolph, presided over the Continental Congress in our nation's beginning—that a Southerner, Thomas Jefferson, wrote the Declaration of Independence, that a Southerner, George Washington, is the Father of our Country—that a Southerner, James Madison, authored our Constitution, that a Southerner, George Mason, authored the Bill of Rights and it was a Southerner who said, "Give me liberty—or give me death," Patrick Henry.

Southerners played a most magnificent part in erecting this great divinely inspired system of freedom—and as God is our witness, Southerners will save it.

Let us, as Alabamians, grasp the hand of destiny and walk out of the shadow of fear—and fill our divine destination. Let us not simply defend—but let us assume the leadership of the fight and carry our leadership across this nation. God has placed us here in this crisis—let us not fail in this—our most historical moment.

You that are here today, present in this audience, and to you over this great state, wherever you are in sound of my voice, I want to humbly and with all sincerity, thank you for your faith in me.

I promise you that I will try to make you a good governor. I promise you that, as God gives me the wisdom and the strength, I will be sincere with you. I will be honest with you.

I will apply the old sound rule of our fathers, that anything worthy of our defense is worthy of one hundred percent of our defense. I have been taught that freedom meant freedom from any threat or fear of government. I was born in that freedom, I was raised in that freedom—I intend to live in that freedom—and God willing, when I die, I shall leave that freedom to my children—as my father left it to me.

My pledge to you—to "Stand up for Alabama," is a stronger pledge today than it was the first day I made that pledge. I shall "Stand up for Alabama," as Governor of our State—you Stand with me—and we, together, can give courageous leadership to millions of people throughout this nation who look to the South for their hope in this fight to win and preserve our freedoms and liberties.

So help me God.

And my prayer is that the Father who reigns above us will bless all the people of this great sovereign State and nation, both white and black.

I thank you.

DWIGHT D. EISENHOWER

"The Domino Theory," April 7, 1954

In the midst of the Battle of Dien Bien Phu, which pitted French imperialists against Vietnamese communists, many wondered if the U.S. would become more involved in the conflict. After being questioned about the situation in a news conference by Robert Richards, a mainstream journalist, President Dwight D. Eisenhower used the phrase "domino theory" to explain his desire to have the United States intervene in French Indochina in order to halt the expansion of communism into other nations of Southeast Asia. The French colony was subsequently divided into Laos, Cambodia, and Vietnam.

SOURCE: *"The President's News Conference of April 7. 1954."* Public Papers of the Presidents of the United States: Dwight D. Eisenhower, *1954, U.S. Government Printing Office, 1960, pp. 382–383.*

Q. ROBERT RICHARDS, COPLEY PRESS: Mr. President, would you mind commenting on the strategic importance of Indochina to the free world? I think there has been, across the country, some lack of understanding on just what it means to us.

THE PRESIDENT. You have, of course, both the specific and the general when you talk about such things.

First of all, you have the specific value of a locality in its production of materials that the world needs.

Then you have the possibility that many human beings pass under a dictatorship that is inimical to the free world.

Finally, you have broader considerations that might follow what you would call the "falling domino" principle. You have a row of dominoes set up, you knock over the first one, and what will happen to the last one is the certainty that it will go over very quickly. So you could have a beginning of a disintegration that would have the most profound influences.

Now, with respect to the first one, two of the items from this particular area that the world uses are tin and tungsten. They are very important. There are others, of course, the rubber plantations and so on.

Then with respect to more people passing under this domination, Asia, after all, has already lost some 450 million of its peoples to the Communist dictatorship, and we simply can't afford greater losses.[1]

But when we come to the possible sequence of events, the loss of Indochina, of Burma, of Thailand, of the Peninsula, and Indonesia following, now you begin to talk about areas that not only multiply the disadvantages that you would suffer through loss of materials, sources of materials, but now you are talking really about millions and millions and millions of people.

Finally, the geographical position achieved thereby does many things. It turns the so-called island defensive chain of Japan, Formosa, of the Philippines and to the southward; it moves in to threaten Australia and New Zealand.

It takes away, in its economic aspects, that region that Japan must have as a trading area or Japan, in turn, will have only one place in the world to go—that is, toward the Communist areas in order to live.

So, the possible consequences of the loss are just incalculable to the free world.

* * *

Q. RAYMOND BRANDT, ST. LOUIS POST-DISPATCH: Mr. President, what response has Secretary Dulles and the administration got to the request for united action in Indochina?

THE PRESIDENT. So far as I know, there are no positive reactions as yet, because the time element would almost forbid.

The suggestions we have, have been communicated; and we will have communications on them in due course, I should say.

Q. ROBERT G. SPIVACK, NEW YORK POST: Mr. President, do you agree with Senator Kennedy that independence must be guaranteed the people of Indochina in order to justify an all-out effort there?[2]

THE PRESIDENT. Well, I don't know, of course, exactly in what way a Senator was talking about this thing.

---

1. Eisenhower is referring to the recent communist conquest of mainland China.

2. John F. Kennedy was serving in the U.S. Senate. Several years later, as president, he would begin U.S. military involvement in Vietnam.

I will say this: for many years, in talking to different countries, different governments, I have tried to insist on this principle: no outside country can come in and be really helpful unless it is doing something that the local people want.

Now, let me call your attention to this independence theory. Senator Lodge, on my instructions, stood up in the United Nations and offered one country independence if they would just simply pass a resolution saying they wanted it, or at least said, "I would work for it." They didn't accept it. So I can't say that the associated states want independence in the sense that the United States is independent. I do not know what they want.

I do say this: the aspirations of those people must be met, otherwise there is in the long run no final answer to the problem.

APPENDIX: ADDITIONAL ROLES (USED IN SOME CLASSES)

Note to Gamemasters: Thirty-five core roles are available from W. W. Norton. If you want to expand your game, additional characters are available through the Reacting Consortium Library. Visit www.reactingconsortiumlibrary.org/ for more information.

ADDITIONAL DELEGATES

Johnson Loyalists

Sen. Walter Mondale (Minn.) filled the senate seat that Hubert Humphrey vacated when he became vice president. For this reason, and others, he is a steadfast supporter of the vice president. He should give a nominating speech for Humphrey.

Mayor Joseph Alioto (Cal.) is the recently elected mayor of San Francisco and is a rising star in the Democratic Party. He is particularly proud of the new Bay Area Rapid Transit system, or BART.

Rep. Ralph Harold Metcalfe Sr. (Ill.) is an Olympic athlete who became a politician from Chicago's predominantly Black and impoverished South Side. He supports the Great Society programs that benefit his constituents and is part of Daley's Chicago machine.

Mayor Carl B. Stokes (Ohio) became one of the first Black mayors of a major U.S. city when he was elected in 1967, but his fortunes have ebbed since Cleveland's Glenville riot killed eleven people and did $2.5 million in damage.

Gov. Richard J. Hughes (N.J.) served as the chair to the credentialing committee that seated Julian Bond while turning away an all-white delegation from Mississippi as well as the noted white supremacist, Gov. Lester Maddox of Georgia. He should give a *second* nomination speech for Humphrey.

TIP

There are two delegates named Hughes. Their positions are quite different.

Doves

Sen. George McGovern (S. Dak.) is a more moderate antiwar Democrat who hopes to acquire Robert Kennedy's supporters in order to steal the presidential nomination from McCarthy and Humphrey.

Gov. Harold Hughes (Iowa) is a progressive Democrat who has grown disenchanted with the Johnson administration and the war in Vietnam; he supports McCarthy and should give a nominating speech for him.

Sen. Abraham Ribicoff (Conn.), a past member of the Kennedy administration, is a progressive Democrat who supports McGovern and should give a nominating speech for him.

Allard Lowenstein (N.Y.) was the leader of the "Dump Johnson" campaign that persuaded McCarthy to challenge Johnson.

Theodore Bikel (N.Y.) is a well-known actor and folk singer. He is a pledge delegate for McCarthy.

Moderates

Sen. Albert Gore Sr. (Tenn.) supports the Great Society and is generally a Johnson loyalist, but he has become utterly opposed to the war in Vietnam.

ADDITIONAL PROTESTERS

Yippies

Bob "Big Man" Lavin is a member of the Headhunters, a northern Illinois motorcycle gang. He does not like authority figures of any kind and is Jerry Rubin's bodyguard. He has been promised drugs and women.

Indeterminates

Hillary Rodham is a college student from Park Ridge, a Chicago suburb. She recently left the Republican Party and is curious about what is happening in Chicago. She told her father that she needed to borrow the car so that she could go see a movie.

Phil Ochs (pronounced "oaks") is a well-known folk singer. He is active in antiwar, civil rights, and union organizing.

Black Activists

Ralph Abernathy is a leader of the nonviolent Southern Christian Leadership Conference (SCLC). He is continuing Martin Luther King Jr.'s work with the Poor People's Campaign.

ADDITIONAL JOURNALISTS

Television Reporters

Haynes Johnson is a reporter for the *Washington Star* and a commentator for NBC News. He won the Pulitzer Prize for his coverage of the Selma March in Alabama. As a commentator for the *Today Show*, he can choose to release his stories in print or on television.

Print Reporters

Russell Baker works for the *New York Times*. His "Observer" column has been critical of Mayor Daley's preparations for the Convention.

David Lewis Stein is a Canadian journalist for the *Toronto Star*. He is particularly interested in the Yippies.

Father Raymond A. Schroth is a liberal Jesuit priest who writes for *America: The National Catholic Review*. He is particularly interested in the motives and ideas of the protesters.

Photographers

These players file images rather than writing or broadcasting stories. They need to submit contact sheets to their editors before assembling the best of their images into a photo essay.

Robert "Bobby" Abbott Sengstacke takes pictures for the *Chicago Defender*, the nation's most renowned Black newspaper. He is determined to counteract the negative images of Black people in the white press.

Radio Journalists

These players create and broadcast audio recordings of their interviews and commentaries. They should coordinate with the GM to figure out the best way to do this.

Studs Terkel has a long-running series of radio interviews on WFMT radio based in Chicago. He is a critic of Mayor Daley and a champion of the working class.

Underground Journalists

John Schultz is known primarily for his fiction writing, which has appeared in the avant-garde *Evergreen Review.*

Norman Mailer writes in the style of New Journalism, which uses literary devices common to fiction when writing nonfiction. He is covering the Convention for *Harper's Magazine.*

Warren Hinckle is the publisher of *Ramparts Magazine.* He plans to publish the *Ramparts Wall Poster* throughout the Convention, and he is soliciting contributions.

Abe Peck is on the staff of *The Seed*, Chicago's most prominent underground newspaper. He is planning on publishing a special Convention issue and welcomes submissions from other journalists.

Buckley vs. Vidal

ABC News decided to pit two of the nation's most acerbic and political wits against each other and to put it on television. These debates between the "left" and the "right" do not settle much of anything, but many find them to be entertaining.

William F. Buckley Jr. is the founder of the *National Review*, the flagship of the modern American conservative movement.

Gore Vidal is a fey, witty essayist, who is determined to skewer Buckley whenever possible.

FILMMAKERS

Large classes can include the cast and crew for the experimental film *Medium Cool.* These players must work together to make a raw short film in the *cinéma vérité* style that uses the Convention and the events surrounding it as a compelling backdrop. They will screen the results during the debriefing session.

Haskell Wexler is a gifted cinematographer. This will be his directorial debut.

Verna Bloom is a young stage actor. This will be her first feature film.

Marianna Hill is an experienced actor who often plays "exotic types" in Hollywood.

Robert Forster is an up-and-coming leading man who worked as a substitute teacher and construction worker in New York before landing a five-picture deal with 20th Century Fox.

SELECTED BIBLIOGRAPHY

In addition to these sources, role-specific sources appear under "To Learn More" or in citations on numerous role sheets.

BOOKS

Anderson, David I. *Vietnamization: Politics, Strategy, Legacy*. Lanham, MD: Rowman & Littlefield, 2020.

Cronkite, Walter. "We Are Mired in Stalemate." In *Reporting Vietnam: Part One: American Journalism 1959–1969*, compiled by Milton J. Bates, Lawrence Lichty, Paul L. Miles, Ronald H. Spector, and Marilyn B. Young, 581–82. New York: Library of America, 1998.

DePaul University Art Museum. *1968: Art and Politics in Chicago*. Chicago: DePaul Art Museum, 2008.

Farber, David. *Chicago '68*. Chicago: University of Chicago Press, 1994.

Gallup, George H. *The Gallup Poll: Public Opinion, 1935–1971*. New York: Random House, 1972.

Gitlin, Todd. *The Sixties: Years of Hope, Days of Rage*. New York: Bantam Books, 1987.

Goodman, Mitchell. *The Movement toward a New America: The Beginnings of a Long Revolution; (A Collage) A What?* New York: Knopf, 1970.

Gould, Lewis L. *1968: The Election That Changed America*. Chicago: Ivan R. Dee, 1993.

Hayden, Tom. "The Streets of Chicago: 1968." In *Writings for a Democratic Society: The Tom Hayden Reader*, 123–55. San Francisco: City Lights, 2008.

Hayden, Tom, Ron Sossi, and Frank Condon. *Voices of the Chicago Eight*. San Francisco: City Lights, 2008.

Kennedy, Edward M. *True Compass*. New York and Boston: Twelve, 2009.

Kusch, Frank. *Battleground Chicago: The Police and the 1968 Democratic Convention*. Chicago: University of Chicago Press, 2008.

Lane, Mark. *Chicago Eyewitness*. New York: Astor-Honor, 1968.

Mailer, Norman. *Miami and the Siege of Chicago: An Informal History of the American Political Conventions of 1968*. Harmondsworth, UK: Penguin, 1969.

Myrus, Donald, ed. *Law & Disorder: The Chicago Convention and Its Aftermath*. Chicago: Donald Myrus and Burton Joseph, 1968.

O'Brien, Justin. *Chicago Yippie! '68*. Mineral Point, WI: Garret Room Books, 2017.

Schneir, Walter, ed. *Telling It Like It Was: The Chicago Riots*. New York: Signet, 1969.

Schultz, John. *No One Was Killed: The Democratic National Convention, August 1968*. Chicago: University of Chicago Press, 1969.

Seale, Bobby, *Seize the Time: The Story of the Black Panther Party and Huey P. Newton*. Baltimore: Black Classic Press, 1996. Originally published by Random House in 1970.

Steigerwald, David. *The Sixties and the End of Modern America*. New York: St. Martin's Press, 1995.

Stein, David Lewis. *Living in the Revolution: The Yippies in Chicago*. Indianapolis and New York: Bobbs-Merrill, 1969.

The Strategy of Confrontation: Chicago and the Democratic National Convention—1968. [Chicago Dept. of Law], 1968.

Walker, Daniel. *Rights in Conflict: Convention Week in Chicago, August 25–29, 1968*. New York: E. P. Dutton, 1968. Originally published by Bantam Books.

White, Theodore H. *The Making of the President, 1968*. New York: Harper Perennial, 2010. Originally published by Atheneum House in 1969.

Zaroulis, Nancy, and Gerald Sullivan. *Who Spoke Up? American Protest against the War in Vietnam, 1963–1975*. New York: Holt, Rinehart, & Winston, 1984.

PERIODICALS

Burns, Clive. "Chicago: A Beautiful but Secret City." *New York Times*, August 26, 1968.

"The Compleat Delegate." *Time*, August 30, 1968.

"Convention of the Lemmings." *Time*, August 30, 1968.

"Daley City Under Siege." *Time*, August 30, 1968. Note: there is a *Chicago Sun-Times* piece by this title too.

Halberstam, David. "Daley of Chicago." *Harper's Magazine*, August 1968, 25–36.

Hardwick, Elizabeth. "Chicago." *New York Review of Books*, September 26, 1968, 5–7.

Janson, Donald. "Holding a Convention in a Garrison City." *New York Times*, August 25, 1968.

Kempton, Murray. "The Decline and Fall of the Democratic Party." *Saturday Evening Post*, November 1968, 19–20, 66–79.

Kenworthy, E. W. "Eugene McCarthy: A Blend of Humility, Arrogance and Humor." *New York Times*, August 30, 1968, 16.

Kifner, John. "On the Road to Chicago with Some Protesters." *New York Times*, August 22, 1968.

Lowenstein, Allard K., and Arnold S. Kaufman. "The Case for Opposing Johnson's Renomination." *War/Peace Report*, November 1967, 12–13.

Lunch, William L., and Peter W. Sperlich, "American Public Opinion and the War in Vietnam." *The Western Political Quarterly* 32, no. 1 (March 1979): 21–44.

Pierson, Robert L. "Behind the Yippies' Plan to Wreck the Democratic Convention." *Official Police Detective Magazine*, December 1968, 8–13, 44–47.

Renov, Michael. "Newsreel: Old and New. Towards an Historical Profile." *Film Quarterly* 41, no.1 (Autumn 1987): 20–33.

"Stalag '68." *Time*, August 2, 1968.

Steinburg, Neil. "The Whole World Watched: 50 Years after the 1968 Chicago Convention." *Chicago Sun-Times*, August 17, 2018.

"Young Dissidents Practice Self-Defense for Chicago Protests." *New York Times*, August 23, 1968.

FILMS

Alk, Howard, dir. *American Revolution II*. Chicago: The Film Group, 1969.

Fruchter, Norman and John Douglas, dir. *Summer '68 (Newsreel #505)*. New York: Newsreel, 1969.

Gazit, Chana, dir. *The American Experience*. Season 8, episode 3, "Chicago 1968." Aired November 13, 1995, on WGBH.

NOTES

For full publication details of the sources cited below, see the Selected Bibliography.

1. The material in this essay is drawn from Stein, *Living in the Revolution*, and three news stories: Kifner, "On the Road to Chicago with Some Protesters"; "Stalag '68"; and "Daley City Under Siege."
2. *Costs and Delivery of Health Services to Older Americans* (U.S. Government Printing Office, 1967) 224.
3. Anderson, *Vietnamization* 14.
4. Cronkite, "We Are Mired in Stalemate" 581–82.
5. Farber, *Chicago '68* 145.
6. Gallup, *The Gallup Poll* 3: 2128.
7. Gallup 3: 2151.
8. Farber 159–60.
9. Farber 172.
10. Farber 174.
11. Farber 175.
12. Farber 178.
13. Farber 179, 181.
14. Farber 182.
15. *The American Experience*, "Chicago 1968."
16. Gallup 3: 2020.
17. Gallup 3: 2043.
18. Gallup 3: 2108.
19. Statistics from Lunch and Sperlich, "American Public Opinion and the War in Vietnam" 25.
20. Gallup 3: 1971–72.
21. Gallup 3: 2124–26, 2135.
22. Gallup 3: 2135, 2153.
23. Mailer, *Miami and the Siege of Chicago* 132.
24. Special thanks to David LaVigne for developing this taxonomy.

ACKNOWLEDGMENTS

Thanks to the team of students who developed in the initial prototype as part of the Game Design Seminar at Simpson College in spring 2012. Dustin McNulty pitched the initial concept and Emily Stover soon joined his efforts. Their initial draft set many of the parameters in terms of documents, roles, and structure. Their teammates Bobby Dennis, JoAnna Freeland, Ryan Stumbo, and Josh Zieman all made significant contributions to this first version of the game. At this point, after years of revision, expansion, and pruning, their prototype is a bit like the first level of Troy, but without it, there would be nothing, so I am particularly grateful for their energy and enthusiasm in the game's initial design.

In the fall of 2013, another section of the Game Design Seminar play-tested a revised version and offered substantive and useful feedback, which reshaped the ways in which demonstrations operate and tightened the issues for discussions of Vietnam policy. Students in the spring 2015 iteration of the course further improved the game. At their insistence, I made journalists more integral, cut a few documents, and added polling data. Their ideas contributed a great deal to the playability of the game. In the fall of 2017, yet another section of the same class helped to sharpen rules related to the operation of the journalists.

In addition to students, a number of others have shaped the game. Christine Lambert, Jon Truitt, and Judy Walden all served as excellent sounding boards at multiple points throughout the game's development. They all cheerfully put up with my ad hoc pondering in a variety of odd settings—driving through rural Iowa, standing in line at the grocery store, waiting for a flight in LaGuardia, etc.

Among the faculty play-testers, Brittany Bayless Fremion and Emily Hess deserve special thanks for their willingness to act as the initial beta testers in 2013–14. Their experiences gave me great confidence in pressing forward with the project. Subsequent feedback from Eric Goddard, John Burney, Neal Allen, Scout Blum, Tracy Lucht, and participants in the 2014 Reacting Game Development Conference at Simpson College were especially important in these early stages. Special thanks to Aaron Vanek, who wrote the role sheet for Hunter S. Thompson and then masterfully inhabited the role during this, his first Reacting conference.

In the fall of 2015 Melissa Blair, Scout Blum, and Andrew Peterson all read the manuscript for the Reacting Editorial Board. Their careful readings encouraged Andrew to orchestrate a run of the game involving multiple sections at the same institution, which encouraged the creation of some additional journalist roles and the further calibration of the mechanics for demonstrations.

Since they become most active in classes that are larger than those I ordinarily have the opportunity to teach, journalist roles have particularly benefitted from the advice of others. Several of Paul Wright's students drafted additional journalist roles.

James Schiffman gave me some great ideas about how to represent journalistic ethics and continued to ask pressing questions as the game continued to develop. David LaVigne created a taxonomy of news stories, and John Giebfried figured out how to improve the operation of the Press Secretaries, who appear in larger games.

The new, improved game was then play-tested by Betsy Powers, John Parrish, Jenn Worth, Andrew Peterson, Amy Tyson, Abby Markwyn, Tony Crider, Aaron Cowan, Abigail Gautreau, and Jonathan Sarris; they all provided high-quality field reports. Taken together, their feedback resulted in a variety of important adjustments and clarifications that make the game work in a wider variety of classroom settings.

Some feedback resulted in particularly dramatic changes. Amy Tyson, Lee Bernstein, and Allison O'Mahen Malcom encouraged further clarification of the rules regarding police action. John Giebfried, Jim Holton, and MaryAnne Christy helped me to fine-tune the Vote Bonus Certificate. Mark Higbee pushed me to revise the admittedly rather sketchy initial version of the Ted Kennedy role. Eric Parks and MaryAnne Christy designed the role-allocation questionnaire, which makes it much easier to match players with roles that they will treasure and fully inhabit. Finally, two of my students, Wade Gibson and Levi Lefebure, contributed even more additional roles.

Much of the ground for using the game in large classes was broken by Jennifer Frost, who ran it several times in sections with around 200 students. She gave me lots of ideas about how to structure the game so that it can be scaled up without great difficulty. If you are playing the game in a large class, thank Jennifer for her bold strides in this direction.

The game also grew because Bill Offutt and Justin Cahill encouraged me to allow the game more class time so that the ideas could blossom more fully. I tried to split the difference by dividing the game into parts, which can be combined into sessions with varying lengths.

Throughout the early years of this process, the hard work of Kristin Graham, who was the interlibrary loan specialist in Simpson College's Dunn Library, greatly deepened and broadened the texts and roles in the game. Her ability to hunt down odd documents and obscure publications is truly a wonder. The fact that once upon a time she was my student only adds to my delight. Linda Sinclair, the administrative assistant for the Humanities Division at Simpson College, also offered her invaluable support.

Toward the end of the game's development, John Burney, the heroic founding chair of the Reacting Consortium's governing board, invited me to run the game with faculty at Doane College, which led to some great conversation and another set of tweaks. Mark Carnes and Jenn Worth decided to add the game to the schedule at the 2019 Reacting Summer Institute at Barnard College. In addition to being great fun, this identified a number of important edits. So many edits! There are good reasons why these games take years to develop.

Finally, W. W. Norton's Justin Cahill, Angie Merila, Katharine Ings, and Thea Goodrich helped me to get the manuscript over the finish line. I hope you enjoy the results. Thanks to all!

CREDITS

Black Panthers: From *The Black Panther* by David Hilliard. Copyright © 2007 by David Hilliard. Reprinted with permission of Atria Books, a division of Simon & Schuster Inc. All rights reserved.

Harris, Dave: "The Assumptions of the Draft," in *The Movement Toward a New America: The Beginnings of a Long Revolution*, ed. Mitchell Goodman. Reprinted with permission, United Church Press.

Hayden, Casey and Mary King: "Sex and Caste," as published in *Liberation* (April 1986 issue). Reprinted by permission of the authors.

Hayden, Tom: Excerpts from *The Port Huron Statement* (Students for a Democratic Society, 1964). Reprinted by permission of the Estate of Tom Hayden.

Hoffman, Abbie: "Media Freaking," *TDR/The Drama Review* 13, no. 4 (Summer 1969): 46–51. © 1969 by The Drama Review. Reproduced by permission of MIT Press Journals.

Lorence, Akmed: Transcript from *No Vietnamese Ever Called Me Nigger*. Directed by David Loeb Weiss (Cinema Guild, 1968). Transcribed by Linda Sinclair. Reproduced by permission of The Cinema Guild, Inc.

Nixon, Richard: Courtesy of the Richard Nixon Foundation.

CPSIA information can be obtained
at www.ICGtesting.com
Printed in the USA
LVHW061942071222
734742LV00007B/300